FRENCH REGIONAL COOKERY

BURGUNDY

FRENCH REGIONAL COOKERY

BURGUNDY

Réné Emin

HAMLYN

Series consultant MARIE-PIERRE MOINE, editor of
TASTE magazine

Editor Diana Craig
Art Editor Lisa Tai
Copy Editors Barbara Croxford, Jenni Fleetwood,
Anne Johnson
Designer Mike Leaman
Picture Researcher Gale Carlill
Production Controllers Mandy Innes, Helen Seccombe

Introduction written by Kate Whiteman
Translation of French material Lesley Bernstein,
Madeleine Johnson
Special Photography Jan Baldwin, Clive Streeter
Food Preparation Linda Fraser, Dolly Meers,
Lyn Rutherford
Styling Maria Kelly, Marion Price

The publishers would like to thank the following for their
kind permission to reproduce the following photographs:
Tony Stone Worldwide pages 6-7; Topham Picture Library
page 9

Half-title page picture: Pâté de Foies de Canard/Flan au
Lard; title page picture: Matelote d'Anguilles/Écrevisses à la
Nage

First published in 1990 by The Hamlyn Publishing Group
Limited
a division of the Octopus Publishing Group
Michelin House
81 Fulham Road
London SW3 6RB

ISBN 0 600 56734 6

Produced by Mandarin Offset

Printed in Hong Kong

CONTENTS

INTRODUCTION

Think of Burgundy and you think of conviviality, for this is an area of fine wine, good eating and joviality. Yet only a small part of this large region of France is given over to the vineyards for which the region is so justly famous.

Much of the area is wooded hills, at the bottom of which lie fertile valleys through which flow the Seine, the Saône and the Yonne. To the west stands the magnificent rocky granite Morvan district at the edge of the Massif Central, a stark contrast to the fertile plains and cool valleys. All these different geographical features are exploited to the full, with wonderful produce, both living creatures and crops, being cultivated where they grow best.

The character of the Burgundian people is as diverse as the region itself, but they have one thing in common – they are proud to belong to this most historic province, where Stone Age settlers came fifteen thousand years ago and which has seen a bloody, warlike series of events – three centuries of Roman rule, then the arrival of the Burgundian tribes, followed by the Huns, then the Saracens. Gradually, over the years, Burgundy became a centre of Christianity and great abbeys, like that at Cluny, were built. For 500 years, Cluny remained the largest and most influential church in Christendom, until St. Peter's was built in Rome.

During these medieval times, the church exerted an enormous religious and artistic influence over the region and remained immensely rich and powerful until Napoleon finally broke up its lands.

By the 14th century, Burgundy had become an independent dukedom with an entirely feudal system. The powerful dukes built glorious châteaux and enjoyed a lifestyle of staggering hedonism and opulence in the premier duchy of France. But the Burgundian tradition of good living began long before the ducal days; Dijon, the capital of the region, was already a gastronomic centre in Roman times. The world's first gastronomic fair was held there and in the 6th century BC, the chronicler Gregory of Tours was already boasting about the magnificent wines of the region. Even today, the people of Burgundy delight in celebrating the glories of their local wine and food. This is a land of plenty.

Although the Burgundian dukes were finally defeated by the French crown in the 16th century, the area has always maintained its individual

Above *A fairytale picture of rural Burgundy: a centuries-old farmhouse overlooks lush meadows, where cows graze by the side of a stream*

character and regional patriotism. *'Je suis fier d'etre bourguignon'* (I am proud to be Burgundian) goes an ancient drinking song and, indeed, the Burgundians seem to revel in the riches of their region. Very few ever move to other areas. Why should they, when their land has so much to offer?

Every part of the region is rich in some kind of produce: succulent Charolais beef are raised on the plains, while the less fertile Morvan is full of every kind of game. There are snails and wild mushrooms in the woods and even truffles, although these are not considered to be quite as fine as those from Périgord.

The rivers and streams hold wonderful fish, including freshwater crayfish, and the white-fleshed poultry (*poulets de Bresse*) is among the best in the world. There is an abundance of fruits in the orchards – cherries and blackcurrants, from which *cassis* is made and, of course, the vines.

FOOD

All this makes Burgundy a gourmet's paradise. The keynote of Burgundian cooking is the combination of food and wine, most notably in dishes like *Boeuf Bourguignon* and *Coq au Vin* and oxtail or ham *des vignerons* – the very names seem to conjure up the scents of the wine cellar. There is an all-purpose red wine sauce, *meurette*, used for everything from partridge to perch.

The cooking is full-flavoured and robust, making the most of the abundant produce of the region. Portions are always generous and are usually accompanied by a pool of rich, dark wine sauce, studded with tiny glazed onions and cubes of fat salt pork.

Dijon, the capital, is rightly noted for its aromatic mustard, made with sour grape juice, which is considered to be the very finest. Its pickled gherkins are delicious, too, and groceries have stacks of colourful assorted pickled vegetables, beautifully arranged in layers in decorative glass jars. *Cassis* is made here, from the succulent blackcurrants of the region, which are also used in *cassissines*, little blackcurrant bonbons and fondants.

For those with a sweet tooth, Burgundy offers a host of delights – nougat from Nevers, aniseed sweets from Flavigny, wonderful fruit tarts and jams and the famous gingerbread-like *Pain d'Epices* from Dijon.

Each area of the region has some new gastronomic delight to offer. There are fat snails and frogs' legs, crayfish cooked in cream, parslied hams in white wine jelly and fish from the rivers and streams. Cream plays a large part in Burgundian cooking and is often combined with white wine to make a sauce for *poulet*, *écrevisses* or *brochet* (pike) *à la crème*. There is a cream flan called *Fouée*, a kind of quiche filled with fat bacon and sprinkled with walnut oil and *saupiquet* – Morvan ham cooked in a brown sauce with local cream. Fish soup, *Pochuse*, is more like a stew, with a medley of fish poached in wine and cream.

Game abounds in Burgundy and is served stuffed with local truffles or casseroled in rich, purplish wine sauces. Often it seems that the food is there simply to complement the wine. This is certainly true of the cheeses of Burgundy, which make a perfect match with fine red wine. Most famous of all is Epoisses, which is regularly washed with *marc de Bourgogne* to develop its powerful flavour and scent. There are goat cheeses, too, some mild and fresh, others like *chèvre de Macon* with a smell so evil that only the bravest soul would dare to eat it!

WINES

All this wonderful food, however, really only serves as an excuse to drink the wines of which Burgundians are so proud and which are among the greatest in the world. The vineyards, grown on dry stony soil, are spread between four main wine-producing areas – the Côte d'Or to the north, The Côtes Chalonnaise and Maconnaise in the centre and the Côte de Beaujolais in the south. The great region of Chablis north of the Côte d'Or is not technically in Burgundy, but Burgundians regard the glorious white wine as their own!

The very finest wines come from the historic Duchy of Burgundy and are generally named after the villages (or, in the case of the Grands Crus, the actual vineyards) in which the vines are grown. These names bring a smile of delight to every lover of wine – Gevrey-Chambertin, Corton-Charlemagne, Romanée-Conti, Montrachet.

Most of the vineyards are owned by several or many different owners, some of whom still like to tend their vines in the old, traditional way. The growers make their own wine, which is usually bottled on the estate where it was grown, thus ensuring the highest possible quality. As a result, much Burgundy wine is expensive. The reds are a deep ruby colour with a fine bouquet; the whites

are mainly full-flavoured and dry and less fragrant than those from Beaujolais.

The best wines, those from the Côte d'Or, are divided into three categories; *village*, (which is better than most ordinary table wines) *premier cru* (first growth) and *grand cru*, which denotes the epitome of viniculture. The northern part of the area, the Côte de Nuits, produces the well-known Nuits St. Georges as well as Napoleon's favourite red wine, Romanée-Conti. The southern half of the area is the Côte de Beaune, where glorious white wines are produced, as well as fine reds – Montrachet, Corton-Charlemagne and Meursault all come from this area. Some of these are so expensive that few people can afford them.

Wines from the Côtes Chalonnaise and Macon-

Above The corn-fed chickens of Bresse are a prized local speciality, renowned for their quality all over France

naise are generally less astronomically expensive. Pouilly-Fuissé comes from this area, which is better known for its whites than its reds. Technically in Burgundy, there are also the very different Beaujolais wines, which are fresh and should be drunk young, although not perhaps quite as young as some *Beaujolais Nouveau*. All complement the food of Burgundy; all contribute to the good living of the area. Why not go to Burgundy and visit some of the *maisons des vins?* You will find it a most rewarding experience.

SOUPS

Burgundian cooks are as imaginative in the making of soup as in their other skills, and this chapter lists just a few of their delicious creations – such as hearty farmhouse fillers like *Soupe au Lard*, substantial enough to form a meal on its own, or smooth and delicately flavoured creams like *Potage au Potiron*, elegant enough to please the most sophisticated palette.

SOUPE AU LARD
BACON SOUP

SERVES 6-8
3 litres (5¼ pints) chicken stock or water
12-16 rashers lean bacon
225 g (8 oz) pork hock
2 large onions, peeled and cut into large dice
3 carrots, peeled and quartered
3 leeks, washed and sliced
2 white turnips, peeled and roughly chopped
2 cloves garlic, chopped
1 green cabbage, chopped
1 bouquet garni
2 cloves
pinch salt
8 white peppercorns, crushed
6-8 slices cottage loaf or French bread

1 Put the stock or water in a large saucepan. Add the bacon and pork hock. Bring to the boil, lower the heat and simmer for 10 minutes, skimming the top regularly.

2 Add the vegetables, bouquet garni, cloves, salt and peppercorns. Cook for 2 hours 20 minutes, then check the seasoning.

3 Put a slice of bread on individual soup plates. With a slotted spoon, remove the meat from the pan and chop it finely. Put a small amount of meat on each slice of bread. Divide the vegetables between the bread slices, then pour over the stock. Serve at once.

POTAGE À L'OSEILLE
SORREL SOUP

SERVES 4-6
250 g (9 oz) sorrel
25 g (1 oz) butter
1 large onion, peeled and finely sliced
500 g (1 lb) potatoes, peeled and quartered
salt and pepper
1 chicken stock cube
2.5 litres (4½ pints) water
2 egg yolks
200 ml (⅓ pint) double cream

1 Thoroughly wash the sorrel, then slice it roughly.

2 Melt the butter in a large saucepan. Add the onion and sweat for 5 minutes over moderate heat until golden. Add 200 g (7 oz) of the sorrel and cook, stirring, for 2-3 minutes. Add the potatoes with salt and pepper to taste. Crumble in the stock cube. Pour in the water, bring to the boil, lower the heat and simmer for 45 minutes.

3 Cool slightly, then purée the sorrel mixture in a food processor or blender. Return the soup to the pan, reheat and check the seasoning.

4 Combine the egg yolks and cream in a small bowl. Remove the soup from the heat and add the egg and cream mixture, stirring. Return to a gentle heat and cook, stirring until the soup thickens slightly; do not let it boil. Finely chop the remaining sorrel. Pour the soup into a tureen, garnish with the finely chopped sorrel, and serve.

P OTAGE AU POTIRON *(ABOVE, RECIPE PAGE 13)*
POTAGE À L'OSEILLE

SOUPE AU CHOU

SOUPE AU CHOU
CABBAGE SOUP

SERVES 4-6
100 g (4 oz) butter
5 rashers lean bacon, diced
1 large onion, peeled and sliced
3 carrots, peeled and diced
1 green cabbage, sliced
100 g (4 oz) young leeks, washed and finely
sliced
225 g (8 oz) potatoes, peeled and diced
salt and pepper
1 clove garlic, finely chopped
2 litres (3½ pints) chicken stock or water
4 egg yolks
200 ml (⅓ pint) double cream

1 Melt the butter in a large saucepan. When hot, add the bacon and fry for 4-5 minutes. Add the onion, carrots, cabbage and leeks and sweat for about 5 minutes.

2 Add the potatoes, salt and pepper to taste, garlic and stock. Cook for 35 minutes over moderate heat.

3 Combine the egg yolks and cream in a small bowl. Remove the soup from the heat and stir in the egg and cream mixture.

4 Return the soup to a gentle heat and cook, stirring until the mixture thickens slightly; do not let it boil or it may curdle. Serve at once.

POTAGE AU POTIRON
PUMPKIN SOUP

SERVES 4-6
500 g (1 lb) pumpkin
100 g (4 oz) butter
1 large onion, peeled and sliced
200 g (7 oz) potatoes, peeled and roughly
chopped
pinch ground nutmeg
salt and pepper
20 g (¾ oz) sugar
1.5 litres (2½ pints) water
1 litre (1¾ pints) milk
200 ml (⅓ pint) double cream
3 slices bread, crusts removed
10 sprigs fresh chervil, chopped, to garnish
100 g (4 oz) Gruyère cheese, grated (optional)

1 Cut the pumpkin into slices, take off the skin and remove the seeds and fibre. Cut the flesh into large cubes.

2 Melt 50 g (2 oz) of the butter in a large saucepan. Add the onion, pumpkin and potatoes, then the nutmeg, 2 teaspoons salt, a pinch of pepper and the sugar. Finally, pour in the water and milk. Bring to the boil over high heat, then lower the heat and simmer for 45-50 minutes.

3 Cool slightly, then purée the pumpkin mixture in a food processor or blender. Return the soup to the pan, reheat and check the seasoning. Add the cream over very low heat; do not allow the soup to boil.

4 Meanwhile cut the bread into 1 cm (½ inch) cubes. Melt the remaining butter in a frying pan and gently fry the bread cubes until golden.

5 Pour the soup into a tureen. Add the chervil and croûtons at the last moment. Sprinkle with the Gruyère cheese if using.

The range of Burgundian hors-d'oeuvre is wide, with dishes to suit every taste and occasion. There are pâtés, puddings and other delicacies made from ham, pork and liver, such as the celebrated *Jambon Persillé*, savoury pastries like *Tourtière Bourgogne* and, finally, those two dishes which, for many, typify the French kitchen – snails and frogs' legs – here scented with Pernod-flavoured butter and accompanied by a smooth parsley and cream sauce respectively.

JAMBON PERSILLÉ
JELLIED HAM WITH PARSLEY

SERVES 6-8
2.5 kg (5½ lb) York ham
1 kg (2 lb) veal knuckle
1 calf's foot, split along the bone
500 ml (18 fl oz) good white Burgundy
1 bouquet garni
2 sprigs fresh tarragon
2 cloves garlic, peeled but left whole
4 carrots, peeled
2 large onions, peeled but left whole
2 leeks, halved and washed
10 white peppercorns, crushed
1½ tablespoons wine vinegar
¾ tablespoon chopped fresh tarragon
¾ tablespoon chopped fresh parsley
¾ tablespoon chopped fresh chervil
JELLY:
1 large carrot, peeled
1 leek, washed
3 egg whites, beaten
2 leaves gelatine
salt and pepper

1 Place the ham, veal knuckle, calf's foot, wine, bouquet garni, sprigs of tarragon, garlic, carrots, onions, leeks and peppercorns in a large saucepan. Cover with water, at least 2-3 cm (1 inch) above the bones. Bring to the boil, lower the heat, cover and simmer for 3 hours.

2 When cooked, take out the ham, calf's foot and knuckle. Remove the flesh from the bones with a fork. Cut the ham and veal into very small dice. Set aside.

3 Pass the stock through a muslin cloth or fine sieve, then return to the clean pan. Bring back to the boil over very high heat and cook, uncovered, for 45 minutes to reduce the stock. Cool slightly.

4 Make the jelly. Finely chop the carrot and leek in a food processor. Put into a bowl and add the egg whites. Transfer to a saucepan, add 600 ml (1 pint) of the lukewarm stock and stir well. Bring back to the boil over low heat, stirring constantly. As soon as boiling point is reached, stop stirring: a crust will form as the stock boils and any particles will pass through the whites and clarify the stock. Boil for 10 minutes, then very gently pass the stock through a fine sieve into a bowl. Add the gelatine and allow to melt. Check the seasoning and set aside to cool.

5 Place the chopped veal and ham in a large glass salad bowl. Stir in the vinegar, chopped tarragon, parsley and chervil. Add the jelly, still slightly warm, stirring well. Cool in the refrigerator for about 12 hours.

6 Cut the jellied ham into slices to serve. The remainder of the stock may be used for a soup such as vermicelli.

JAMBON PERSILLÉ *(ABOVE)*
GÂTEAU DE FOIES DE VOLAILLE *(BELOW, RECIPE PAGE 17)*

RIGODON *(ABOVE)*
CRÉPINETTES AUX CHÂTAIGNES *(BELOW)*

GÂTEAU DE FOIES DE VOLAILLE
BAKED CHICKEN LIVERS

SERVES 4

400 g (14 oz) chicken livers
salt and pepper
pinch ground nutmeg
2 eggs, separated
2 cloves garlic, finely chopped
125 g (4½ oz) butter
125 g (4½ oz) plain flour
750 ml (1¼ pints) milk

1 Finely chop the livers to a paste. Add salt, pepper and nutmeg to taste, then stir in the egg yolks and garlic.

2 Melt the butter in a saucepan and add the flour. Gradually add the milk. then simmer gently over low heat for 20 minutes, stirring frequently.

3 Add the livers to the sauce, mixing well. Whisk the egg whites until stiff, then add to the sauce, folding in gently.

4 Butter a large oven-proof ramekin dish or mould and pour in the liver mixture. Cook in a preheated moderately hot oven, 200°C (400°F), Gas Mark 6 for 45 minutes. Accompany with a fresh tomato or mushroom sauce if liked.

RIGODON
BAKED HAM PUDDING

SERVES 6

2 litres (3½ pints) milk
12 eggs
4½ tablespoons rice flour
200 g (7 oz) butter
400 g (14 oz) ham or lean belly of pork, cut into small dice
1 bunch chives, chopped, to garnish

1 Bring the milk to the boil in a saucepan. Break the eggs into a bowl. Sprinkle the rice flour on to the eggs, stirring vigorously. Add the milk, stirring constantly.

2 Melt 150 g (5 oz) of the butter in a saucepan, add the ham and sweat for 4-5 minutes. If using pork, blanch for 3-4 minutes. Drain well, then sweat in the butter. Add the ham or pork to the batter.

3 Grease a large oven-proof mould with half the remaining butter. Pour in the batter and dot with butter.

4 Bake in a preheated moderately hot oven, 190-200°C (375-400°F), Gas Mark 5-6 for 30 minutes. Serve warm, sprinkled with chopped chives.

CRÉPINETTE AUX CHÂTAIGNES
PORK AND SWEET CHESTNUT PARCELS

SERVES 6

750 g (1½ lb) lean pork
3 large shallots, peeled and finely chopped
1½ tablespoons finely chopped fresh parsley
pinch ground coriander
salt and pepper
400 g (14 oz) fresh sweet chestnuts, peeled and finely chopped
2 eggs
1 large pork membrane (from the brain), cut into 5 cm (2 inch) squares
150 g (5 oz) pork dripping or butter
120 ml (4 fl oz) vegetable oil
10 sprigs fresh chervil or chopped chives, to garnish

1 Cut the pork into very small pieces. Place in a bowl with the shallots, parsley, coriander, salt, pepper and sweet chestnuts. Add the eggs and mix well.

2 Place a small ball of the mixture on to one of the squares of membrane and bring the 4 corners together. Repeat the process until all the stuffing is used up. Flatten the balls with a spoon or the palm of your hand.

3 Heat the dripping and oil in a frying pan over high heat. Add the parcels, reduce the heat and fry for about 5-6 minutes on each side until brown. Drain, transfer to a serving dish and garnish with chopped chervil or chives.

PÂTÉ DE FOIES DE CANARD
DUCK LIVER PÂTÉ

SERVES 6
500 g (1 lb) duck livers, cleaned
200 g (7 oz) butter
250 g (9 oz) skinned belly of pork, cut into small dice
50 g (2 oz) smoked ham, cut into small dice
5 cloves garlic, crushed
2 large onions, peeled and roughly chopped
1 small bouquet garni
salt and pepper
1½ tablespoons brandy
4 tablespoons double cream

1 Make sure the duck livers are well cleaned, and that the bile duct (green sac) is removed, otherwise it will make the pâté very bitter.

2 Melt 100 g (4 oz) of the butter in a saucepan over high heat. Add the duck livers and fry for 2-3 minutes. Stir in the pork, ham, garlic, chopped onion, bouquet garni and ¼ teaspoon pepper. Cover and cook over a low heat for 40 minutes, stirring every 5 minutes to prevent burning.

3 Remove the pan from the heat and allow to cool for 10 minutes. Discard the bouquet garni, then purée all the duck liver mixture in a food processor or blender. Add the remaining butter, the brandy and cream. Check the seasoning.

4 Transfer the pâté to a serving dish and put in the refrigerator for at least 20-25 minutes until firm. Serve this pâté with lightly toasted bread. It can also be used as a spread in sandwiches.

FLAN AU LARD
BACON QUICHE

SERVES 6
250 g (9 oz) Pâte Brisée (shortcrust pastry – see method and page 76)
20 g (¾ oz) butter
5-6 rashers smoked bacon, cut into small pieces
6 eggs
750 ml (1¼ pints) single cream or milk
pepper
2 tomatoes, skinned and thinly sliced

1 When making the pastry, follow the normal recipe but use lard instead of butter as this will provide a better flavour. Roll out the pastry and use to line a 25 cm (10 inch) flan or quiche tin.

2 Melt the butter in a frying pan, add the bacon and fry for 2-3 minutes until the bacon is lightly cooked but not browned. With a slotted spoon, remove the bacon and sprinkle into the pastry case.

3 Place the eggs in a bowl with the cream. Add the butter remaining in the frying pan and a pinch of pepper. Beat well and pour over the bacon in the pastry case. Bake in a preheated moderately hot oven, 200°C (400°F), Gas Mark 6 for 35 minutes.

4 When the quiche is cooked, remove from the oven and spread the thinly sliced tomatoes on top of the filling, then return it to the oven for 10 minutes. Serve warm with a green salad.

Pâté de foies de canard (ABOVE)
FLAN AU LARD (BELOW)

T OURTIÈRE BOURGOGNE *(ABOVE)*
CHAMPIGNONS EN BRIOCHE *(BELOW)*

TOURTIÈRE BOURGOGNE
BURGUNDY PORK AND VEAL PIE

SERVES 6
500 g (1 lb) belly of pork
500 g (1 lb) lean veal
200 ml (⅓ pint) white wine
1 bouquet garni
400 g (14 oz) Pâte Brisée (shortcrust pastry –
see page 76)
salt and pepper
pinch ground nutmeg
¾ tablespoon chopped fresh parsley
3 cloves garlic, crushed
6 shallots, peeled and finely chopped
1½ tablespoons brandy
2 eggs

1 The day before, cut the
pork and veal into small dice. Put the wine and
bouquet garni in a large dish, add the meat and
marinate, turning the meat every 2 hours.

2 On the day, make the
pastry 2-3 hours in advance. Leave to rest in a cool
place.

3 Remove the meat from
the marinade and place it in a bowl. Add salt, pepper, nutmeg, parsley, garlic and shallots. Stir in
the brandy and eggs, mixing well.

4 Divide the pastry in
half. On a floured surface, roll out one piece of
pastry and use to line the base and sides of a round
pie dish, pressing well into place. Lay the meat
mixture evenly on the pastry base. Dampen the
pastry edges. Roll out the remaining pastry and
use as a lid. Crimp the edges with 2 fingers to seal.
Make 2 incisions in the top of the pastry with the
point of a knife to release excess steam.

5 Bake in a preheated
moderately hot oven, 190-200°C (375-400°F),
Gas Mark 5-6 for 50 minutes. Serve hot or cold.

CHAMPIGNONS EN BRIOCHE
BRIOCHE WITH MUSHROOMS

SERVES 4
Pâte à Brioche (see page 76)
butter and flour for coating
100 g (4 oz) butter
4 large shallots, peeled and finely chopped
1 clove garlic, finely chopped
350 g (12 oz) button mushrooms, wiped and
sliced
salt and pepper
2 teaspoons brandy
200 ml (⅓ pint) double cream
½ teaspoon chopped fresh chervil

1 Make the brioche
dough. Lightly butter 4 baba moulds or similar
tins (as a last resort one larger mould will do), dust
with flour and shake out the excess. Fill each
mould three-quarters full with the dough. Make a
small cross in the centre of the dough with a knife.
Bake in a preheated moderate oven, 200°C
(400°F), Gas Mark 6 for 30 minutes.

2 Melt the butter in a
saucepan, add the shallots and garlic and sweat for
a few minutes. Add the mushrooms and sweat for a
further few minutes. Add salt and pepper to taste,
then stir in the brandy and cream. Reduce over
moderate heat until the cream coats the back of a
spoon. Check the seasoning and add the chervil.

3 When the brioches are
cooked, remove from the moulds. With the point
of a knife, cut a 'lid' from the top of each brioche.
Remove some of the dough and divide the mushroom mixture between the brioches. Replace the
lids and return to the oven for about 2 minutes to
warm through.

GRENOUILLES PERSILLÉES
FROGS' LEGS WITH PARSLEY AND CREAM SAUCE

When buying frogs' legs, make sure they are fresh, (check by smelling them), and that the flesh is firm.

SERVES 4

32-40 frogs' legs, depending on size
200 g (7 oz) plain flour, plus ½ tablespoon
salt and pepper
300 g (11 oz) butter, plus ½ tablespoon
4 shallots, peeled and chopped
1 clove garlic, chopped
200 ml (⅓ pint) dry white Burgundy
750 ml (1¼ pints) double cream
2 teaspoons chopped fresh parsley

1 Wash the frogs' legs well in lightly vinegared water to rid them of any impurities. Dry well with a cloth or paper towels.

2 Put 200 g (7 oz) of the flour on a large plate. Season the frogs' legs with 2 teaspoons salt and a pinch of pepper, then roll them in the flour, shaking off the excess.

3 Melt 300g (11 oz) of the butter in a large frying pan over high heat. When the butter turns nutty brown, add the frogs' legs. Lower the heat to moderate and cook for 5-6 minutes on each side. Remove the frogs' legs from the pan using a slotted spoon and keep warm in a dish.

4 If necessary, pour off some of the melted butter from the pan. Heat the remaining butter, add the shallots and garlic and fry gently over low heat, stirring constantly. Add the wine and reduce over high heat by a quarter. Combine the remaining butter and flour in a small bowl and mix well. Stir the cream into the pan. When the sauce boils, add the butter and flour mixture (*beurre manié*), a little at a time, stirring with a wooden spoon or whisking to prevent the formation of lumps. Check the seasoning.

5 Add the frogs' legs to the sauce and reheat for 1 minute. Stir in the chopped parsley, then transfer to a serving dish and serve.

ESCARGOTS À LA BOURGUIGNONNE
SNAILS, BURGUNDY STYLE

Snail dishes may be china or metal. They have indentations that hold the snails securely during cooking.

SERVES 4

48 snails and their shells
250 g (9 oz) butter
3 shallots, peeled and finely chopped
3 cloves garlic, finely chopped
2 teaspoons finely chopped fresh parsley
2 teaspoons finely chopped fresh chervil
salt and pepper
2 tablespoons lemon juice
½ teaspoon Pernod or Ricard

1 Place the snail shells in a saucepan of slightly salted water and boil for 7 minutes. Drain well and put on a baking sheet. Heat in a preheated moderately hot oven, 200°C (400°F), Gas Mark 6 for 5 minutes to evaporate any remaining water. Leave to cool.

2 Soften the butter in a bowl. Add the shallots, garlic, parsley, chervil, salt and pepper to taste, lemon juice and Pernod and mix thoroughly.

3 When the shells are cold, put a small amount of the butter mixture into each shell followed by a snail, then seal with more butter. Repeat this process until all the snail shells are filled.

4 Put the filled snail shells into china or metal snail dishes, with the filling uppermost to prevent the butter running out during cooking. Increase the oven temperature to 220°C (425°F), Gas Mark 7 and cook for about 7-8 minutes, but do not let the snails dry out. Serve the snails immediately with chunks of bread to soak up the buttery juices.

Escargots à la bourguignonne

EGGS AND CHEESE DISHES

Burgundy is famed for its wines and what better partner for them than cheese? To exploit this natural affinity, Burgundian cooks have created several cheese-based dishes, like *Beignets au Fromage* to drink with a white Burgundy, or *Fromage Fort* to drink with a red. Eggs may not seem to have the same compatability as cheese, but they can make a surprisingly happy marriage with wine as in, for instance, *Oeufs Pochés à la Bourguignonne* or *Oeufs Cocotte à la Dijonnaise*.

OEUFS COCOTTE
EGGS IN RAMEKINS

SERVES 4 or 8
100 g (4 oz) butter
4 shallots, peeled and finely chopped
200 g (7 oz) button mushrooms, wiped and
sliced
1 slice cooked York ham, finely chopped
1 tomato, skinned, seeded and finely chopped
salt and pepper
8 eggs
4½ tablespoons single cream
8 sprigs fresh chervil, to garnish

1 Melt 75 g (3 oz) of the butter in a saucepan. Add the shallots and fry until golden. Stir in the mushrooms, ham and tomato, adding a pinch each of salt and pepper. Cook for about 5 minutes. Cool slightly.

2 Grease 8 ramekin dishes with the remaining butter. Divide the mixture between the dishes, filling a third of each dish. Carefully break an egg into each dish, avoiding breaking the yolks.

3 Put the ramekins into a roasting pan and add sufficient water to come halfway up the sides of the dishes. Cover with a lid or foil and bring to the boil over moderate heat. Lower the heat and simmer for 8-10 minutes; the eggs are cooked when the whites are firm and the yolks have a glazed appearance.

4 Take the ramekins from the pan and, just before serving, put a little cream on top of the eggs. Garnish each dish with a sprig of chervil.

OEUFS POCHÉS À LA BOURGUIGNONNE
POACHED EGGS IN RED WINE SAUCE

SERVES 4
1.5 litres (2½ pints) red wine
salt
8 white peppercorns, crushed
3 cloves garlic, crushed
1 small bouquet garni
8 eggs
8 slices French bread
2 teaspoons butter
2 teaspoons plain flour

1 Put the wine in a large saucepan. Add a pinch of salt, the peppercorns, 2 cloves garlic and the bouquet garni. Bring to the boil, lower the heat and simmer for 7-8 minutes. Strain the wine into a bowl, then return to the clean pan and reheat.

2 When the red wine is boiling, break each egg on to a plate to check for freshness and to avoid breaking the yolks in the liquid. Slide each egg into the wine and poach for 3 minutes.

3 Toast the slices of French bread and rub each slice with the remaining garlic. When the eggs are poached, place one on each slice of bread.

4 Combine the butter and flour in a small bowl and mix well. Add to the wine, a little at a time, stirring or whisking well to prevent the formation of lumps. Check the seasoning. Strain the sauce over the eggs through a fine sieve, then serve.

OEUFS COCOTTE *(LEFT)*
OEUFS POCHÉS À LA BOURGUIGNONNE *(RIGHT)*

OEUFS COCOTTE À LA DIJONNAISE *(ABOVE)*
OMELETTE MORVANDIOTE *(BELOW)*

OEUFS COCOTTE À LA DIJONNAISE
BAKED EGGS DIJON-STYLE

SERVES 6
150 g/5 oz butter
1 slice ham, preferably cooked on bone, chopped
100 g (4 oz) button mushrooms, wiped and chopped
3 shallots, peeled and finely chopped
salt and white pepper
1 teaspoon Dijon mustard
6 tablespoons white Burgundy
1 tablespoon chopped fresh tarragon
1 tablespoon chopped fresh chervil
6 tablespoons double cream
12 eggs

1 Melt 100 g (4 oz) of the butter in a saucepan over gentle heat. Add the chopped ham and mushrooms and stir for 2-3 minutes. Add the shallots, allow to sweat for 4-5 minutes, then season with salt and pepper. Stir in the mustard. Stir well and add the white wine. Allow to reduce over high heat until there is virtually no liquid left. Then add the chopped herbs and cream, and reduce by three-quarters.

2 Butter 12 ramekin dishes using 15 g (½ oz) of the remaining butter, and divide the prepared mixture between them. Carefully break an egg on top of each dish, avoiding breaking the yolks. Place the ramekins in a roasting pan and add sufficient water to come halfway up the sides of the dishes. Cover with a lid or foil. Bring the water to the boil, then lower the heat and simmer for about 10 minutes, or until the eggs are ready. The egg whites should be solid but the yolks still runny.

3 Just before serving, dot each of the ramekins with a small knob of the remaining butter.

OMELETTE MORVANDIOTE
OMELETTE MORVAN-STYLE

This is traditionally made in a single pan, as in the recipe below. If, however, you do not have a very large omelette pan, make 4 individual omelettes instead.

SERVES 4
12 eggs
salt and white pepper
100 g (4 oz) butter
1 small onion, peeled and roughly chopped
300 g (11 oz) smoked ham, such as Parma, finely sliced into julienne
150 g (5 oz) button mushrooms, wiped and sliced if large
250 ml/8 fl oz double cream.
1 tablespoon chopped fresh chervil to garnish

1 Break the eggs into a large bowl. Season with salt and pepper and beat well with a fork for 2-3 minutes.

2 In a large omelette pan, melt the butter over low heat. Add the onion and ham. Allow to sweat for 4-5 minutes, then add the mushrooms and cook gently for a further 2-3 minutes.

3 Add the cream to the eggs and stir well. Then pour the mixture over the ham and mushrooms in the pan. Allow to cook for 3-4 minutes, lifting the sides of the omelette to allow any uncooked mixture to flow underneath.

4 When the underside of the omelette is cooked, place a large plate on top of the omelette pan and turn upside down. Slide the omelette back into the pan, the cooked side now facing upwards, and cook for a further 3-4 minutes.

5 Transfer the omelette to a large serving dish and sprinkle with chopped chervil. Serve on its own or with a mixed salad and new or sautéed potatoes.

BEIGNETS AU FROMAGE
CHEESE FRITTERS

SERVES 6
8 egg whites
200 g (7 oz) Emmenthal or Gruyère cheese, grated
2 litres (3½ pints) oil for deep frying

1 Whisk the egg whites in a large bowl until stiff. Incorporate the grated cheese, using a wooden spoon and folding the mixture gently from top to bottom to avoid making it heavy.

2 Heat the oil to 180-190°C (350-375°F) or until a cube of bread browns in 30 seconds.

3 With the aid of a teaspoon form the cheese and egg mixture into small balls, each the size of a walnut. Use a second spoon to slide these carefully into the hot oil. Leave for 4-5 minutes over a moderate heat, turning the fritters regularly. Drain on paper towels and serve immediately, accompanied by glasses of white Burgundy.

FROMAGE FORT À LA BEAUJOLAISE
POTTED MIXED CHEESES

This dish must be made 10-12 days in advance.

SERVES 6
2 leeks, washed
200 ml (⅓ pint) water
salt and pepper
50 g (2 oz) mature goats' milk cheese, grated
50 g (2 oz) mature cows' milk cheese
(Mozzarella or feta cheese are good substitutes), grated
100 g (4 oz) Bleu d'Auvergne, Bleu de Bresse or Roquefort, crumbled
175 ml (6 fl oz) dry white wine
1 tablespoon Marc de Bourgogne
25 g (1 oz) butter, softened

1 Place the leeks in a saucepan with the water. Add salt to taste. Bring to the boil, then simmer for about 15 minutes. Drain the leeks, reserving the cooking stock.

2 Combine all the cheeses in a large glass bowl, add most of the stock, the white wine, Marc and salt and pepper to taste. Mix thoroughly until a soft, easy-to-spread paste is obtained. Cover well with foil and put in a warm place for about 10-12 days. Do not disturb.

3 After 10-12 days, remove the foil, stir again, then add the butter. Serve spread on slices of bread.

GOUGÈRE
CHEESE CHOUX RING

SERVES 4-6
150 g (5 oz) plain flour
250 ml (8 fl oz) water
100 g (4 oz) butter
salt and pepper
4 eggs
50 g (2 oz) Gruyère cheese, grated
40 g (1½ oz) Gruyère cheese, in thin strips
butter and flour for greasing

1 Sift the flour on to a sheet of greaseproof paper. Put the water into a saucepan with the butter and a pinch of salt. Heat gently until the butter melts, then bring to the boil. Remove the pan from the heat and shoot in all the flour. Beat vigorously. Return to the heat and beat until the mixture forms a ball.

2 Off the heat, add the eggs, beating well between each addition. At the same time, gradually incorporate the grated cheese and pepper. Finally work in half the sliced cheese.

3 Have ready a jug of hot water and a greased and floured baking sheet. Using a tablespoon dipped in the hot water, place spoonfuls of the pastry on to the baking sheet to form a circle. Cut the remaining Gruyère into small pieces and dot on top of the choux ring.

4 Bake in a preheated moderate oven, 180°C (350°F), Gas Mark 4 for 30 minutes until well risen, crisp and golden.

FROMAGE FORT À LA BEAUJOLAISE *(ABOVE)*
BEIGNETS AU FROMAGE *(BELOW)*

FISH AND SHELLFISH

Burgundy is surrounded by land on all sides, but this does not prevent the discerning Burgundian from savouring delicious fish and shellfish, the fruits of the region's rivers. Pike, that freshwater predator, appears in several guises, from featherlight *Quenelles de Brochet* to fillets poached in a cream and wine sauce. Trout and eel feature, too, combined with mushrooms and wine, while *écrevisses* – freshwater crayfish – are served simply, in all their solitary splendour, needing only chunks of bread to mop up the cooking juices.

QUENELLES DE BROCHET
PIKE QUENELLES

SERVES 6

150 g (5 oz) skinned and filleted pike
500 ml (18 fl oz) fish stock
150 g (5 oz) plain flour
250 ml (8 fl oz) water
100 g (4 oz) butter
salt and pepper
2 egg yolks
pinch grated nutmeg
SAUCE:
500 ml (18 fl oz) crème fraîche
25 g (1 oz) butter
100 g (4 oz) shallots, finely chopped
500 g (1 lb) mushrooms, wiped and roughly chopped
juice of 1 lemon
2 egg yolks

1 Place the fish in a saucepan. Add the fish stock. Bring to the boil, lower the heat and simmer very gently for about 15 minutes or until the fish flakes easily when tested with the tip of a knife. With a slotted spoon, transfer the fish to a blender or food processor and work to a purée. Reserve the fish stock in the saucepan.

2 Sift the flour on to a sheet of greaseproof paper. Put the water into a saucepan with the butter and a pinch of salt. Heat gently until the butter melts, then bring to the boil. Remove the pan from the heat and shoot in all the flour at once. Beat vigorously. Return the pan to the heat and continue to beat until the mixture forms a ball, leaving the sides of the pan clean.

3 Off the heat, whisk in the egg yolks, one at a time. Season with pepper and nutmeg. Whisk again, then add the pike purée, mixing lightly but thoroughly.

4 On a generously-floured work surface, roll the quenelles dough lightly into a sausage shape. Cut into 10 cm (4 inch) lengths and shape into dumplings.

5 Bring a large saucepan of salted water to the boil. Have ready a large bowl of cold water. Add the quenelles to the boiling water, a few at a time. As each quenelle rises to the surface, remove it with a slotted spoon and transfer to the bowl of cold water, then drain on a tea towel for at least 2 hours.

6 Meanwhile make the sauce. Add the crème fraîche to the saucepan containing the fish stock and mix well. Place over moderate heat and reduce slightly. Melt the butter in a frying pan, add the shallots and sweat until soft. Stir in the mushrooms and lemon juice and cook until all the liquid has evaporated. Stir into the crème fraîche mixture.

7 Arrange the quenelles in a single layer in an ovenproof dish. Transfer 5 tablespoons of the sauce to a bowl and beat in the egg yolks. Stir the mixture back into the sauce. Pour the sauce over the quenelles and bake in a preheated moderately hot oven, 200°C (400°F), Gas Mark 6 for about 15 minutes until all the quenelles are well risen. Serve at once.

QUENELLES DE BROCHET

FILLETS DE BROCHET À LA DIJONNAISE *(ABOVE)*
ESTOUFFADE DE BROCHET *(BELOW)*

FILETS DE BROCHET À LA DIJONNAISE
FILLETS OF PIKE DIJON-STYLE

SERVES 6-8
1 pike, weighing about 2 kg (4½ lb), filleted
6 shallots, peeled and finely chopped
3 bay leaves
1 small bunch thyme
1 small sprig tarragon
salt and pepper
3 tablespoons Marc de Bourgogne
3 tablespoons Noilly Prat
1 litre (1¾ pints) white Montrachet
50 g (2 oz) butter
50 g (2 oz) pork dripping
300 g (11 oz) small button mushrooms, wiped
1 teaspoon Dijon mustard
200 ml (⅓ pint) single cream
1 tablespoon chopped fresh chervil
1 tablespoon chopped chives

1 Soak the fillets of pike in cold running water to remove any impurities.

2 Place the fillets in a large bowl with the shallots, bay leaves, thyme, tarragon, salt and pepper, Marc, Noilly Prat and white wine. Cover the mixture and marinate in the refrigerator for 24 hours.

3 Put the butter and pork dripping on the base of a large, deep flameproof dish. Arrange the fillets of fish on top with the skin sides facing down. Pour the marinade on top and add the mushrooms. Cook in a preheated hot oven, 230°C (450°F), Gas Mark 8, for 20 minutes, basting every 5-7 minutes.

4 Lift out the fillets, using a slotted spoon. Take care not to break them. Transfer to a serving dish and keep warm.

5 Add the mustard to the stock and allow to reduce over high heat for 2-3 minutes. Lower the heat, add the cream and simmer for a few minutes more, until the sauce coats the back of a spoon. Check the seasoning.

6 Pour the sauce over the fish and garnish with chervil and chives.

ESTOUFFADE DE BROCHET
PIKE STEW

SERVES 6
2 small pike, each weighing about 575 g (1¼ lb)
175 g (6 oz) butter
6 shallots, peeled and finely chopped
3 cloves garlic, finely chopped
1 bouquet garni
salt and pepper
1 bottle white Burgundy
1 litre (1¾ pints) fish stock
175 ml/6 fl oz Marc de Bourgogne
25 g (1 oz) plain flour
3 tablespoons double cream
2 egg yolks
1 tablespoon chopped fresh tarragon to garnish

1 Ask your fishmonger to clean and gut the fish. Remove the head and tail, which may be used to make the fish stock. Then slice across the fish, making cutlets about 4-5 cm (1½-2 inches) thick. The fish cutlets should be thick enough to not to fall apart when cooked.

2 Melt 150 g/5 oz of the butter in a flameproof casserole over high heat. Add the shallots, garlic and bouquet garni, lower the heat and allow to sweat gently for 4-5 minutes. Add the fish and cook for a further 6-7 minutes, checking from time to time and shaking the pan to prevent scorching. Season with salt and pepper and add the white wine, fish stock and Marc.

3 Bring to simmering point, cover and simmer over low heat for 15 minutes. With a slotted spoon, carefully transfer the fish to a serving dish and keep warm. Allow the stock to reduce by a third. Meanwhile mix the remaining butter and the flour in a bowl. Add this mixture (*beurre manié*) to the sauce a little at a time, whisking well. Simmer for about 3 minutes, then check the seasoning.

4 Mix the cream and egg yolks in a bowl. Remove the sauce from the heat and stir in the egg and cream mixture. Pour the sauce over the fish and garnish with chopped tarragon. Serve with steamed new potatoes and a fresh green vegetable of your choice.

TRUITE DE RIVIÈRE
RIVER TROUT

SERVES 4
40 button onions
175 g (6 oz) butter, plus 1 teaspoon
½ teaspoon caster sugar
1½ tablespoons water
300 g (11 oz) button mushrooms, wiped
salt and pepper
4 × 200 g (7 oz) river trout
1 litre (1¾ pints) red wine
450 ml (¾ pint) fish stock
1 bouquet garni
2 tablespoons chopped chives to garnish
SAUCE:
150 g (5 oz) butter, plus 2 teaspoons
4 shallots, peeled but left whole
1 beef stock cube, crumbled
2 teaspoons plain flour
2-3 drops liquid gravy browning (optional)

1 Soften the skins of the button onions by soaking them in warm water for 10 minutes. Slip off the skins. Bring a saucepan of water to the boil, add the onions and cook for 10 minutes. Drain thoroughly and pat dry on paper towels.

2 Melt 100 g (4 oz) of the butter in the clean saucepan and add the onions. Sauté for 3-4 minutes until golden brown, then stir in the sugar and water and simmer for about 10 minutes or until the water has reduced and the onions are coated in a shiny glaze. Set the saucepan aside.

3 Melt 50 g (2 oz) of the remaining butter in a frying pan, add the mushrooms and cook over gentle heat for 5 minutes, stirring to make sure that they are evenly done. Stir in salt and pepper to taste. Set the frying pan aside.

4 With the remaining butter, generously grease the base of a flameproof oval earthenware or enamel casserole, large enough to take the trout in a single layer. Arrange the trout in the casserole and pour over the wine and fish stock. Season with salt and pepper and add the bouquet garni. The liquid should cover the fish – if not, add more wine and fish stock. Place the casserole over moderate heat and cook the trout for 12 minutes.

5 Meanwhile prepare the sauce. Melt 150 g (5 oz) of the butter in a small saucepan, add the shallots and cook over gentle heat for 5 minutes.

6 Press the mixture through a fine sieve into a bowl. Return the purée to the clean saucepan, add the stock cube and cook over moderate heat, stirring frequently until the purée has reduced by two-thirds.

7 Mix the remaining butter with the flour in a small bowl. Add this mixture (*beurre manié*) to the shallot purée, a little at a time, whisking constantly until a smooth sauce is formed. If a deeper colour is preferred, add the gravy browning.

8 Return the onions and mushrooms to the heat and warm through gently. Transfer the trout to a serving platter and pour the sauce over. Garnish by arranging the mushrooms on one side of the dish and the onions on the other. Sprinkle the chives over the centre of the trout and serve immediately.

TRUITE DE RIVIÈRE

MATELOT D'ANGUILLES *(ABOVE)*
ÉCREVISSES À LA NAGE *(BELOW)*

MATELOTE D'ANGUILLES
EELS IN WINE

SERVES 4

100 g (4 oz) butter, plus 2 teaspoons
4 medium eels, cleaned and cut into 10 cm
(4 inch) lengths
salt and pepper
2 large onions, peeled and thickly sliced
4 cloves garlic, crushed
3 carrots, peeled and thickly sliced
½ fennel heart, finely sliced
1 bouquet garni
3 teaspoons brandy
1 litre (1¾ pints) good red wine
450 ml (¾ pint) fish stock
2 teaspoons plain flour
2-3 drops liquid gravy browning (optional)
15-20 button onions, peeled but left whole
225 g (8 oz) mushrooms, wiped and quartered
croutons and chopped fresh parsley to garnish

1 Melt 50 g (2 oz) of the butter in a large frying pan over moderate heat. Add the eels, with salt and pepper to taste. Cover the pan and cook gently for 5 minutes.

2 Stir in the onions, garlic, carrots and fennel, with the bouquet garni, brandy, wine and fish stock. Cook, covered, for 30-45 minutes

3 With a slotted spoon, transfer the eels to a casserole and keep warm.

4 Mix 2 teaspoons of the remaining butter with the flour. Remove the bouquet garni from the frying pan and add the butter and flour mixture (*beurre manié*) a little at a time, whisking to make a smooth sauce. Deepen the colour with a few drops of gravy browning, if liked.

5 Melt the remaining butter in a small frying pan, add the button onions and cook over moderate heat for 4-5 minutes. Using a slotted spoon, transfer the onions to the casserole.

6 Add the mushrooms to the butter remaining in the small frying pan and sauté for 2-3 minutes. Using a slotted spoon, transfer to the casserole.

7 Pour the sauce over, arrange the croutons around the edge of the casserole and sprinkle the parsley on top.

ÉCREVISSES À LA NAGE
CRAYFISH IN COURT-BOUILLON

SERVES 6

2 litres (3½ pints) water
1 litre (1¾ pints) white wine
1 litre (1¾ pints) fish stock
3 tablespoons white wine vinegar
2 onions, peeled and roughly sliced
3 carrots, peeled and roughly sliced
10 white peppercorns, crushed
½ teaspoon salt
1 bouquet garni
48 medium freshwater crayfish, gutted and
cleaned
fresh coriander, to serve

1 Combine the water, wine, fish stock and vinegar in a fish kettle or large saucepan. Add the onions, carrots, peppercorns, salt and bouquet garni, bring to the boil and cook for 15 minutes.

2 Add the crayfish, a few at a time, so that the stock continues to boil. Cook for 5 minutes.

3 With a slotted spoon transfer the crayfish to a casserole and garnish with the coriander. Boil the stock until reduced by about half, remove the bouquet garni and pour into a separate cassserole. Each guest spoons a few crayfish into a bowl, adds stock and vegetables, if liked, and eats the crayfish with his fingers. Chunks of bread may be offered to mop up the liquid, and finger bowls should be provided.

MEAT DISHES

Grazing in lush meadows, the white Charolais cattle of Burgundy create a romantic picture – and also produce some of the world's finest beef. Beef features strongly in Burgundian cuisine, and no part of the animal is wasted, whether it be tender young veal, tougher braising steak, oxtail or offal. The same country thrift is also applied to the pig, with dishes made from gammon, bacon and trotter.

CÔTES DE VEAU AUX FINES HERBES
VEAL CHOPS WITH HERBS

SERVES 6
6 veal chops
salt and pepper
150 g (5 oz) butter
1 tablespoon olive oil
4 shallots, peeled and finely chopped
6 tablespoons dry white wine
1 tablespoon chopped fresh parsley
1 tablespoon chopped fresh chervil
1 tablespoon chopped fresh tarragon
1 tablespoon chopped fresh chives
1 teaspoon chopped fresh coriander
SAUCE:
25 g (1 oz) butter
25 g (1 oz) plain flour
500 ml (18 fl oz) vegetable stock
1 chicken stock cube, crumbled
salt and pepper
2 egg yolks, beaten
2 tablespoons double cream

1 First prepare the sauce. Melt the butter in a saucepan, add the flour and stir quickly and thoroughly with a wooden spoon over low heat. Gradually add the stock, stirring to prevent the formation of lumps. Add the chicken stock cube, season with salt and pepper and simmer very gently for about 10 minutes.

2 Meanwhile, season the chops with salt and pepper. Melt the butter with the olive oil in a large frying pan. When hot, fry the veal chops over moderate heat for 6 minutes on each side. Remove the chops from the pan and keep warm.

3 Add the shallots to the pan and sweat for 2-3 minutes. Stir in the white wine, then reduce the liquid by half over high heat, stirring continuously. Add the herbs.

4 Add the shallot and herb mixture to the prepared sauce and remove from the heat. Mix the egg yolks and cream in a bowl. Stir into the sauce, mix well and check the seasoning. Transfer the chops to a serving dish and pour over the sauce. Serve at once.

ENTRECÔTES BOURGUIGNONNES
STEAKS BURGUNDY-STYLE

SERVES 4
4 rump or porterhouse steaks, each weighing
225-250 g (8-9 oz)
salt and pepper
75 g (3 oz) butter
4 shallots, peeled and finely sliced
1 tablespoon Dijon mustard
1 teaspoon chopped fresh coriander
½ bottle white Burgundy
1 tablespoon chopped fresh tarragon to garnish

1 Season the steaks with salt and pepper. Melt the butter in a frying pan over moderate to high heat. When it is hot, add the steaks to the pan and fry for 4 minutes on each side.

2 Add the shallots, mustard and coriander to the pan and stir well. Pour on the white wine and reduce by three-quarters over moderate heat. Check the seasoning and pour the sauce over the steaks. Sprinkle with tarragon and serve at once with chips or sautéed potatoes.

ENTRECÔTES BOURGUIGNONNES *(ABOVE)*
CÔTES DE VEAU AUX FINES HERBES *(BELOW)*

BEOUF BOURGUIGNON

BOEUF BOURGUIGNON
BEEF BOURGUIGNON

SERVES 6

1 kg (2 lb) braising steak, cubed
flour for coating
4 tablespoons butter
150 g (5 oz) unsmoked streaky bacon, cut into
thin strips
24 small onions, peeled but left whole
1 shallot, peeled and chopped
120 ml (4 fl oz) cognac
175 ml (6 fl oz) beef stock
500 ml (18 fl oz) good red wine
1 bouquet garni
salt and pepper
pinch quatre epices
1 clove garlic, crushed
150 g (5 oz) small button mushrooms, wiped
1 tablespoon plain flour
chopped parsley to garnish

1 Toss the cubed steak in flour, shaking off the excess. Set aside. Melt 2 tablespoons of the butter in a large flameproof casserole. Add the bacon and onions and fry until the onions are golden. With a slotted spoon, remove the bacon and onions and reserve.

2 Add the floured steak to the fat remaining in the casserole. Seal the meat over moderate heat, then add the shallot and mix well. Pour on the cognac and ignite it. Tip the pan carefully to ensure that all the alcohol burns. When the flames die down, add the stock and wine, with the bouquet garni. Season with salt, pepper and quatre epices. Stir in the garlic. Lower the heat, cover the casserole and simmer gently for 1¾ hours.

3 Melt 1 tablespoon of the remaining butter in a small frying pan. Add the mushrooms and brown gently. With a slotted spoon, transfer the mushrooms to the casserole. Add the reserved bacon and onions and continue to simmer for 20 minutes more.

4 Just before serving, mix the remaining butter with the flour. Stir this mixture (*beurre manié*), a little at a time, into the casserole, to thicken the sauce.

5 Serve the beef bourguignon from the casserole or pour it into a heated serving dish. Sprinkle with chopped parsley and serve with steamed potatoes.

FOIE DE VEAU CHAROLAIS
CHAROLAIS CALF'S LIVER

SERVES 4

575 g (1¼ lb) calf's liver
salt and pepper
150 g (5 oz) butter
1 tablespoon oil
3 shallots, finely chopped
6 tablespoons Marc de Bourgogne or good
brandy
120 ml (4 fl oz) white wine
200 ml (⅓ pit) double cream
1 tablespoon chopped fresh parsley, to garnish

1 Ask your butcher to skin the liver and thinly slice. (Removing the skin avoids excessive shrinking of the liver and prevents curling during cooking.) Sprinkle the liver with salt and pepper; do not use flour.

2 Heat the butter and oil in a pan over high heat. Add the liver and fry for 2 minutes each side. Transfer the liver to a serving dish and keep warm.

3 Add the shallots to the fat remaining in the pan, then after a few seconds add the Marc. Pour in the wine and simmer until reduced by half. Add the cream, bring to the boil, then simmer over moderate heat until the sauce is reduced by half.

4 Check the seasoning. Coat the liver with the sauce and garnish with chopped parsley.

ENTRECÔTES CHAROLAISES
CHAROLAIS STEAKS

SERVES 6
175 g (6 oz) butter
6 sirloin steaks, each weighing about 225-250 g
(8-9 oz)
salt and pepper
3 shallots, peeled and finely chopped
2 cloves garlic, crushed
100 g (4 oz) button mushrooms, wiped and
quartered
1 beef stock cube, crumbled
300 ml (½ pint) red wine
25 g (1 oz) plain flour
1 tablespoon chopped fresh chervil to garnish

1 Melt 150 g (5 oz) of the butter in a large frying pan over high heat. Season the steaks with salt and pepper and, when the butter is very hot, add the steaks to the pan and fry for 5 minutes on each side.

2 Remove the meat from the pan and keep warm. Add the shallots to the pan and allow to sweat for 2-3 minutes. Then add the garlic and mushrooms, and cook gently for about 7-8 minutes over moderate heat. Sprinkle on the beef stock cube, pour over the red wine and cook for a further 5 minutes.

3 Combine the remaining butter with the flour. Add this mixture (beurre manié) to the sauce a little at a time, stirring constantly with a wooden spatula to blend thoroughly. Simmer gently for a further 5 minutes. Check the seasoning and pour over the steaks. Garnish with chopped chervil and serve at once.

QUEUE DE BOEUF À LA VIGNERONNE
OXTAIL WITH GRAPES

SERVES 6
100 g (4 oz) butter
3 tablespoons olive oil
3 oxtails, cut into pieces
2 large onions, peeled and sliced
3 carrots, peeled and cut into
5 cm/2 inch lengths
1 stick celery, cut into 5 cm/2 inch lengths
1 tablespoon salt
1 teaspoon pepper
75 g (3 oz) plain flour
3 tablespoons cognac or brandy
1 bottle good-quality white Burgundy
3 litres (5¼ pints) beef stock or water
1 bouquet garni
GARNISH:
2 large bunches seedless white grapes, washed
50 g (2 oz) butter
1 tablespoon chopped chives

1 Heat the butter and oil in a large saucepan over high heat. Add the oxtail pieces and fry for about 10 minutes until golden. Add the onions, carrots and celery and fry gently for about 5 minutes. Sprinkle the salt, pepper and flour over the meat and mix well. Cook for 1-2 minutes, then add the cognac, wine and beef stock, with the bouquet garni.

2 Cover the pan and cook gently for about 3 hours, stirring occasionally to prevent sticking. If the liquid evaporates too quickly, add some water.

3 Meanwhile, cut the grapes in half. Melt the butter in a frying pan over moderate heat. Add the grapes and stir for about 4-5 minutes.

4 When the meat is tender, add the grapes and heat through for 5 minutes. Check the seasoning. Transfer to a serving dish and sprinkle with chopped chives. Serve at once.

ENTRECÔTES CHAROLAISES *(ABOVE)*
QUEUE DE BŒUF À LA VIGNERONNE *(BELOW)*

43

POTÉE BOURGUIGNONNE
BURGUNDY HOT POT

SERVES 6
800 g (1¾ lb) corner gammon
a small piece of forehock or gammon knuckle
50 g (2 oz) dried green or white haricot beans
1 pig's trotter
16 rashers lean smoked bacon
2 cervelas (or smoked Polish sausage)
1 bouquet garni
2 large onions, peeled and quartered
10 carrots, halved if large, peeled
8 whole baby turnips, peeled
5 leeks, washed and halved if large
4 cloves garlic, peeled but left whole
1 large green cabbage, quartered
15 white peppercorns, crushed
8 large potatoes, peeled and roughly chopped
MUSTARD SAUCE:
stock (see method)
50 g (2 oz) butter
50 g (2 oz) plain flour
5 tablespoons Dijon mustard
1 tablespoon wine vinegar
salt and pepper
3 tablespoons double cream
4 egg yolks

1 The day before cooking, soak the gammon and forehock in cold water for about 12-15 hours. Change the water several times to rid the meat of most of its salt content. Soak the dried beans overnight in sufficient cold water to cover.

2 The next day, put all the meat, except the cervelas, in a very large saucepan and cover completely with cold water. Do not add any salt. Bring to the boil and cook over high heat for 30 minutes.

3 Drain the beans and add to the pan with the bouquet garni, onions, carrots, turnips, leeks, whole garlic cloves, cabbage and peppercorns. Bring the meat and vegetables to the boil, then lower the heat and simmer gently for about 1 hour.

4 Prick the cervelas with a fork to prevent bursting and add to the pan with the potatoes. Make sure both meat and vegetables are well covered with liquid. Cook over moderate heat for 30 minutes more. Turn off the heat, cover the pan with a lid and leave on the stove to keep warm until it is nearly time to serve and you are ready to make the sauce.

5 About 10 minutes before serving, make the sauce. Strain 1 litre (1¾ pints) of the stock from the saucepan into a measuring jug, leaving the remaining stock in the covered pan. Melt the butter in a clean saucepan over moderate heat. Add the flour, mix well and cook over gentle heat for 2-3 minutes, stirring to prevent any lumps forming.

6 Gradually add the measured stock, mixing quickly and thoroughly with a wooden spoon to prevent the formation of lumps. Cook gently for about 5 minutes, then stir in the mustard and vinegar with salt and pepper to taste. Add the cream, mixing well. Remove from the heat and whisk in the egg yolks. (Because this is a delicate egg sauce, do not reheat or it may curdle.)

7 With a slotted spoon transfer the meat from the potée to individual deep plates and surround with vegetables. Serve the mustard sauce separately. Any meat left over can be reheated the next day. Any remaining broth may also be reheated and poured over slices of bread in individual soup bowls, then sprinkled with grated cheese.

J AMBON DU MORVAN AUX PETITS LÉGUMES *(ABOVE, RECIPE PAGE 47)*
POTÉE BOURGUIGNONNE *(BELOW)*

POT-AU-FEU BOURGUIGNON

JAMBON DU MORVAN AUX PETITS LÉGUMES
GAMMON WITH DICED VEGETABLES

SERVES 6
1 × 1.5 kg (3½ lb) gammon joint
2 large onions, peeled and quartered
4 carrots, peeled
2 sticks celery, halved
1 bouquet garni
10 black peppercorns, crushed
3 cloves
225 g (8 oz) mushrooms, wiped and sliced
200 ml (⅓ pint) Madeira

1 Put the gammon in a large saucepan with sufficient cold water to cover. Put the lid on, bring the water to the boil, then lower the heat and simmer for 20 minutes.

2 Add the vegetables, bouquet garni, peppercorns and cloves. It is not necessary to add salt as gammon is naturally salty. Bring the stock back to the boil, then lower the heat and simmer for about 1 hour.

3 With a slotted spoon, remove the gammon and vegetables from the pan. Cut the gammon into thick slices and arrange in an ovenproof dish. Dice or roughly chop the cooked vegetables and add to the dish with the mushrooms. Measure 200 ml (⅓ pint) of the gammon stock and add to the dish with the Madeira. Reserve any of the remaining stock for later use in soups or stews.

4 Cook in a preheated hot oven, 220°C (425°F), Gas Mark 7 for 15 minutes. Drain the cooking juices into a saucepan. Transfer the meat to a serving dish and arrange the vegetables on top. Cover with greaseproof paper or foil and keep warm.

5 Bring the cooking juices to the boil, then lower the heat and simmer until they are reduced by half. Pour the juices into a sauce boat.

6 Serve the gammon and vegetables with boiled or mashed potatoes mixed with mashed celery. Hand the sauce separately.

POT-AU-FEU BOURGUIGNON
BURGUNDY POT-AU-FEU

The rich and delicious pot-au-feu stock is often used for vermicelli soup with croûtons. Cabbage soup may also be made with the stock.

SERVES 8
1 kg (2 lb) shin of beef
1 kg (2 lb) chuck or blade steak
1 kg (2 lb) gammon, forehock or collar bacon
1 kg (2 lb) veal knuckle
300 g (11 oz) veal bones, including a marrow bone
3 small onions, peeled but left whole
4 carrots, halved if large, peeled
4 leeks, washed and cut into 5 cm/2 inch lengths
8 small turnips, peeled
4 tomatoes, skinned
2 sticks celery
1 bouquet garni
20 peppercorns, crushed
1 clove garlic, unpeeled
2 cloves
2 tablespoons coarse salt

1 Put all the meat and bones in a very large saucepan and cover with cold water (one third above the meat). Bring to the boil, lower the heat and simmer for about 1 hour, occasionally removing any scum that rises to the top of the liquid.

2 Add the vegetables, bouquet garni, peppercorns, garlic and cloves. Cover with a lid and simmer gently for 3 hours more, continuing to skim off any scum. Add the salt and continue to simmer for about 1 hour.

3 With a slotted spoon, remove the meat. Slice or chop it, discarding the bones, and arrange on a large serving dish. Spoon the vegetables around the meat. Pour over a small quantity of the hot stock, to moisten. Serve with pickled gherkins, pickled vegetables and Dijon mustard or a fresh tomato suace. This dish is also excellent with boiled potatoes or rice cooked in the pot-au-feu broth. Any leftover meat may be served cold with a green salad and pickles.

ROGNONS DE VEAU AUX CHAMPIGNONS
VEAL KIDNEYS WITH MUSHROOMS

SERVES 4
575 g (1¼ lb) veal kidneys
salt and pepper
175 g (6 oz) butter
400 g (14 oz) button mushrooms, wiped and quartered
3 tablespoons white wine
1 tablespoon chopped fresh parsley, to garnish
SAUCE:
50 g (2 oz) butter
50 g (2 oz) plain flour
1 litre (1¾ pints) milk
salt and pepper
pinch ground nutmeg

1 Cut the kidneys into quarters and remove the cores. Thinly slice the kidneys, sprinkle with salt and pepper and set aside.

2 Make the sauce. Melt the butter in a saucepan and add the flour, stirring well. Cook for 3 minutes over low heat, stirring. Gradually add the milk, stirring briskly to form a smooth sauce. Stir in salt, pepper and nutmeg to taste. Bring to the boil, then lower the heat and simmer for 10 minutes, stirring constantly.

3 Melt 100 g (4 oz) of the butter in a frying pan over high heat. When it sizzles, add the prepared kidneys and fry for 6-7 minutes, tossing occasionally. Remove the kidneys with a slotted spoon and keep warm. Add the remaining 50 g (2 oz) butter to the fat remaining in the pan. When melted, add the mushrooms with salt and pepper to taste. Cook for 5 minutes. Add the mushrooms and kidneys to the sauce, stirring well over low heat.

4 Add the wine to the frying pan and heat, scraping to incorporate the residue on the base of the pan. Reduce the wine for 1 minute, then add to the kidney and mushroom mixture. Transfer to a serving dish and garnish with chopped parsley.

TRIPES À LA BOURGUIGNONNE
TRIPE, BURGUNDY STYLE

SERVES 6
2 kg (4½ lb) tripe, cut in wide strips
300 g (11 oz) butter, melted
400 g (14 oz) fresh white breadcrumbs
salt and pepper
300 ml (½ pint) walnut oil
BOURGUIGNON BUTTER SAUCE:
300 g (11 oz) butter
4 shallots, peeled and finely sliced
5 cloves garlic, crushed
salt and pepper
1 tablespoon Marc de Bourgogne or good brandy
1 tablespoon Pernod or Ricard
3 tablespoons finely chopped fresh parsley

1 Dip the tripe strips in the butter, then roll them in the breadcrumbs. Add salt and pepper to taste.

2 Heat the oil in a large frying pan. When the oil starts smoking, add about 10-15 strips of tripe at a time and cook over fairly high heat for about 3 minutes on each side until golden. Remove from the heat, transfer the tripe to a serving dish and keep warm.

3 Make the sauce. Melt the butter in a saucepan, add the shallots and sweat over medium heat for 2-3 minutes. Add the garlic, then the remaining ingredients. Stir well, pour over the tripe and serve immediately. (Make sure the butter sauce is very hot, otherwise the dish will be too rich.)

T RIPES À LA BOURGUIGNONNE *(ABOVE)*
ROGNONS DE VEAU AUX CHAMPIGNONS *(BELOW)*

POULTRY AND GAME

P oultry, or more particularly the famed chickens known as *poulets de Bresse*, is a speciality of the region. There are various Burgundian chicken dishes, but the most celebrated has to be *Coq au Vin* in which chicken is exquisitely combined with another regional favourite, red wine. As well as domestic poultry, there is game such as rabbit, hare and partridge from the woods and fields, and these may be gently fried in butter, then simmered in wine to create a succulent casserole, like *Lapin en Meurette* or *Civet de Lièvre*.

COQ AU VIN
CHICKEN IN WINE

SERVES 4

1 × 2 kg (4½ lb) chicken
50 g (2 oz) butter
5 rashers bacon, cut in strips
1 onion, peeled and chopped
3 cloves garlic, crushed
1 bouquet garni
175 ml (6 fl oz) Marc de Bourgogne or good brandy
20 small white onions, peeled but left whole
1 teaspoon salt and a pinch of pepper
2 tablespoons plain flour
1 tablespoon tomato purée
1 bottle good-quality red Burgundy
200 ml (⅓ pint) water
GARNISH:
2 large slices soft white bread, crusts removed
50 g (2 oz) butter
1 tablespoon chopped fresh chervil

1 Cut the chicken into serving portions. Melt the butter in a large heavy-bottomed saucepan over moderate heat, add the chicken and fry on all sides until golden brown. Using a slotted spoon, transfer the chicken portions to a plate and reserve.

2 Add the bacon to the fat remaining in the pan and fry, stirring, for 3-4 minutes. Stir in the chopped onion and garlic and fry for 1 minute more, then add the bouquet garni. Pour over the Marc and stir thoroughly, scraping the base of the pan to incorporate any sediment.

3 Ignite the Marc. When the flames die down, return the chicken to the pan with the white onions, salt and pepper. Sprinkle the flour over the chicken, stir well and add the tomato purée, wine and water. Bring to the boil, stirring constantly. Lower the heat, cover the pan and simmer for 40-45 minutes, stirring the sauce occasionally.

4 Meanwhile prepare the garnish. Cut each slice of bread in half diagonally to form 2 triangles. With a sharp knife, shape each triangle into a heart, with the point of the triangle forming the tip of the heart. Melt the butter in a frying pan over moderate heat, add the hearts and fry until golden on both sides. Drain on paper towels. Place the chopped fresh chervil in a shallow bowl.

5 When the chicken is tender, transfer it to a large heated platter with the onions. Pour the sauce over the top. Holding each fried bread heart by its tip, dip it in the sauce and then in the chopped chervil. Stand the hearts upright between the chicken portions and serve at once, with new potatoes, rice or boiled noodles, if liked.

COQ AU VIN

POUSSINS DE LOUHANS GRAND-MÈRE *(ABOVE)*
POULE BOUILLIE À LA BOURGUIGNONNE *(BELOW, RECIPE ON PAGE 54)*

POUSSINS DE LOUHANS GRAND-MÈRE
ROAST POUSSINS

SERVES 4
4 × 400 g (14 oz) poussins
1 teaspoon each salt and pepper
50 g (2 oz) butter
1 tablespoon cooking oil
175 ml (6 fl oz) Noilly Prat
120 ml (4 fl oz) dry white Burgundy
STUFFING:
4 tablespoons milk
25 g (1 oz) fresh or canned truffles, roughly
chopped, with can juices reserved
3 slices soft white bread, crusts removed
4 teaspoons butter
2 rashers bacon, diced
poussin livers (see method)
3 shallots, peeled and finely chopped
2 cloves garlic, crushed
¼ teaspoon fresh thyme
salt and pepper
2 egg yolks
200 ml (⅓ pint) Marc de Bourgogne

1 Remove the livers from the poussins and reserve. Clean all the body cavities thoroughly.

2 Make the stuffing. Pour the milk into a shallow dish with the can juices from the truffles, if available. Add the bread and set aside to allow the bread to soak in the liquid and to soften.

3 Melt the butter in a small frying pan over high heat. Add the bacon and sauté for 2-3 minutes. Stir in the reserved poussin livers, with the chopped shallots, crushed garlic and thyme. Fry, stirring occasionally, for 5 minutes more.

4 Transfer the mixture to a blender or food processor, add salt and pepper to taste and process for a few seconds only – do not over-process: the texture should be thick and rough.

5 Remove the bread from the milk mixture, squeeze out and discard the excess liquid and crumble the bread into a large bowl. Stir in the liver mixture and mix well. Add the egg yolks, the chopped truffles and the Marc. Mix thoroughly and add more salt and pepper if required.

6 Fill the poussin cavities lightly with the stuffing, closing the openings with a poultry needle threaded with fine string. Season the birds with salt and pepper.

7 Melt the butter in the oil in a flameproof roasting pan. Add the poussins and fry over high heat until golden brown on all sides. Transfer the roasting pan to a preheated moderately hot oven, 200°C (400°F), Gas Mark 6 and roast for 20-30 minutes or until all the poussins are cooked.

8 Return the roasting pan to the top of the stove. Remove the poussins to a serving platter and keep warm while preparing the sauce. Pour the Noilly Prat and white wine into the pan, scraping the base to loosen any sediment and stirring vigorously to incorporate it into the wine mixture. Cook the sauce over moderate heat, stirring continuously, until the liquid has reduced by half.

9 To serve, remove the string closures on the poussins and spoon a portion of stuffing on to 4 individual plates. Add a poussin to each, pour over the sauce and serve very hot, accompanied by small roast potatoes or Dauphine potatoes if liked.

POULE BOUILLIE À LA BOURGUIGNONNE
BOILED CHICKEN, BURGUNDY-STYLE

SERVES 4
1 × 2.5 kg (5½ lb) firm boiling fowl
2 tablespoons coarse salt
1 bottle white Burgundy
2 large onions, peeled and quartered
4 carrots, peeled and cut into large chunks
2 sticks celery, cut into 5 cm (2 inch) lengths
8 small turnips, peeled
2 chicken stock cubes, crumbled
15 black peppercorns, crushed
4 cloves
1 bouquet garni
40 g (1½ oz) butter
50 g (2 oz) plain flour
1 tablespoon chopped fresh parsley to garnish

1 Place the boiling fowl in a large saucepan and add water to cover the bird by one third. Add the salt and bring to the boil. Partially cover the pan and boil for 5 minutes, skimming off the scum with a metal spoon as it rises in the pan. Lower the heat and simmer for 25 minutes more.

2 Add the wine and vegetables with the stock cubes, peppercorns, cloves and bouquet garni. Allow the cooking liquid to return to the boil, then lower the heat and simmer for about 1 hour or until the chicken is tender.

3 Remove the chicken from the pan and keep it warm until required. Reserve the stock and vegetables, discarding the bouquet garni.

4 Combine the butter and flour in a small bowl and mix well to form a *beurre manié*.

5 Strain 1 litre (1¾ pints) of the cooking liquid into a second saucepan and heat to just below the boiling point. Add the *beurre manié* a little at a time, whisking constantly, to form a smooth sauce. Check seasoning and cook, stirring, for 5 minutes. Reheat the vegetables in the remaining stock.

6 Cut the chicken into neat portions and arrange on a serving dish. Using a slotted spoon, transfer the vegetables to the dish and pour the sauce over. Serve at once, garnished with parsley. The remaining stock may be used to cook 100 g (4 oz) pilaf rice to serve with the meat.

LAPIN EN MEURETTE
RABBIT IN WINE SAUCE

SERVES 4
2 × 1.25 kg (2½ lb) rabbits, skinned and cleaned
salt and pepper
50 g (2 oz) butter plus 1 teaspoon
2 onions, peeled and chopped
1 tablespoon plain flour
200 ml (⅓ pint) vegetable stock
200 ml (⅓ pint) chicken stock
200 ml (⅓ pint) dry white wine
1 bouquet garni
120 ml (4 fl oz) double cream
3 egg yolks
4 tablespoons lemon juice
1 tablespoon chopped fresh chervil, to garnish

1 Cut the rabbits into neat portions and sprinkle with salt and pepper. Melt 50 g (2 oz) of the butter in a large saucepan, add the rabbit portions and fry over high heat until browned on all sides. Add the onions, lower the heat and sweat for 3-4 minutes.

2 Sprinkle the flour over the rabbit portions, mix well and add the vegetable stock, chicken stock, wine and bouquet garni. Cook gently for 1½ hours, stirring occasionally to prevent sticking.

3 Meanwhile, place the remaining butter in a bowl with the cream, egg yolks and lemon juice. Mix well.

4 When the rabbit is cooked, transfer the portions to a heated serving dish and keep warm. Remove the bouquet garni from the pan juices, add the cream mixture and whisk over gentle heat until the sauce thickens. Adjust the seasoning. Pour the sauce over the rabbit, sprinkle with chervil and serve.

LAPIN EN MEURETTE

PERDREAUX À LA MODE BOURGUIGNONNE

PERDREAUX À LA MODE BOURGUIGNONNE
PARTRIDGES, BURGUNDY-STYLE

SERVES 4

4 medium partridges

salt and pepper

2 rashers streaky bacon, halved lengthways

175 g (6 oz) butter plus 1 teaspoon

1 teaspoon plain flour

24 small white onions, peeled but left whole

225 g (8 oz) firm button mushrooms, wiped

200 ml (⅓ pint) Marc de Bourgogne or good brandy

120 ml (4 fl oz) good red wine

3 tablespoons well-seasoned chicken stock

1 tablespoon chopped fresh chervil, to garnish

1 Clean the body cavities of the partridges thoroughly and sprinkle with salt and pepper. Wrap a strip of bacon around each bird, securing with string or strong thread.

2 Melt 100 g (4 oz) of the butter in a large frying pan. Add the partridges and fry over high heat until browned on all sides. Cover the pan with a lid or foil, lower the heat and cook for about 15 minutes or until the partridges are cooked. Mix 1 teaspoon of the remaining butter with the flour in a small bowl and set aside.

3 Meanwhile bring a small saucepan of water to the boil, add the onions and blanch for 2-3 minutes. Immediately drain the onions and cool under running water for 3-4 minutes. Drain thoroughly. Repeat the process with the mushrooms. Reserve.

4 Melt the remaining butter in a second frying pan, add the blanched onions and fry for 5 minutes. Add salt and pepper to taste and keep warm over very low heat.

5 As soon as the partridges are cooked, transfer them to a serving dish with a slotted spoon and keep warm. Add the Marc to the pan in which the partridges were cooked and stir vigorously, scraping the base of the pan to incorporate any sediment. Stir in the red wine and chicken stock and cook for 5-6 minutes.

6 Add the butter and flour mixture *(beurre manié)* a little at a time, whisking to form a smooth sauce. Check seasoning and cook, stirring, for 3 minutes more. Add the onions and mushrooms and cook for 2 minutes.

7 To serve, remove the string closures on the partridges, pour over the sauce and sprinkle with chervil. Serve at once.

LAPIN À LA MOUTARDE
RABBIT WITH MUSTARD

SERVES 4

1 saddle of rabbit, cut into serving portions

2 tablespoons oil

25 g (1 oz) butter, flaked

4 large shallots, peeled and chopped

120 ml (4 fl oz) dry white wine

300 ml (½ pint) crème fraîche

4 tablespoons Dijon mustard

salt and pepper

1 Arrange the rabbit portions in a shallow ovenproof dish, sprinkle with the oil and dot with flakes of butter. Cook in a preheated moderately hot oven, 200°C (400°F), Gas Mark 6 for 30 minutes, turning once, until golden brown.

2 Sprinkle on the shallots, add the wine and return to the oven for a further 45 minutes, basting frequently.

3 Combine the mustard and crème fraîche in a bowl. Season lightly with salt and pepper and mix well. Pour over the rabbit and cook for 15 minutes more. Serve at once.

CIVET DE LIÈVRE AU CHAMBERTIN
JUGGED HARE WITH CHAMBERTIN

It is essential to choose a hare in prime condition for this recipe. It should be purchased before being skinned. Look for a shiny coat, short nails, dark nose, short regular teeth, and ears that are firm and springy.

SERVES 6
1 × 2.25 kg (5 lb) hare
150 g (5 oz) butter
1 tablespoon olive oil
salt and pepper
2 tablespoons plain flour
1 tablespoon tomato purée
3 shallots, peeled and finely chopped
3 cloves garlic, crushed
1 tablespoon Marc de Bourgogne
4 rashers bacon, diced
225 g (8 oz) button mushrooms, wiped
20 small white onions, peeled but left whole
1 tablespoon each finely chopped chives and
fresh chervil, to garnish
MARINADE:
1 large onion, peeled and finely sliced
3 cloves garlic, crushed
10 black peppercorns, crushed
1 bouquet garni
200 ml (⅓ pint) cognac or brandy
2 bottles Chambertin or good quality red
Burgundy

1 Ask your butcher to skin and clean the hare, cutting it into pieces and reserving the liver (without the gall). Mix all the ingredients for the marinade in a shallow dish large enough to hold all the hare portions (except the liver) in a single layer. Add the hare, mix well, cover with cling film and marinate in the refrigerator for 24 hours, turning the meat over several times.

2 Drain the hare, reserving the marinade, and pat dry on paper towels. Melt 100 g (4 oz) of the butter in the olive oil in a large saucepan, add the portions of hare and fry for about 10 minutes or until golden on all sides. Add salt and pepper to taste.

3 Sprinkle the hare portions with flour, stirring to prevent scorching. Stir in the tomato purée, shallots and garlic. Strain the marinade into a jug. Remove the bouquet garni from the strainer and reserve. Gradually add the strained marinade to the saucepan, beating constantly to form a smooth sauce. Add the Marc with the reserved bouquet garni, mix well, cover and simmer for 2-2½ hours.

4 Meanwhile chop the reserved hare liver finely and set aside. Bring a small saucepan of water to the boil, add the bacon and blanch for 2 minutes. Drain thoroughly. Blanch the mushrooms and onions in the same way as the bacon.

5 Shortly before serving, melt the remaining butter in a small frying pan. Add the chopped liver and fry gently, stirring, then remove from the pan. Add the blanched bacon and fry over moderate heat for 5 minutes. Add the mushrooms and onions and fry for 5 minutes more.

6 Stir the chopped liver into the hare stew and arrange the portions of hare with the sauce in a deep earthenware serving dish. Scatter the bacon, mushrooms and onions over the top, sprinkle with chives and chervil and serve immediately, accompanied by mashed or boiled potatoes or fresh noodles.

CIVET DE LIÈVRE AU CHAMBERTIN

VEGETABLES

Asparagus, beans, celery, pumpkin, potatoes, leeks – all these vegetables find a place in the cuisine of Burgundy. To appreciate their delicate taste and texture to the full, it is wise not to blur the palette by serving too many other dishes at the same time. Delicacies like *Asperges de Brétigny* should obviously be presented as an individual course, while others, like *Potée de Lentilles Bourguignonne*, are a meal in themselves, needing little accompaniment except good wine, good bread and relaxed company.

ASPERGES DE BRÉTIGNY
ASPARAGUS WITH VINAIGRETTE

SERVES 6
2 tablespoons coarse salt
2 kg (4½ lb) white or mauve asparagus
VINAIGRETTE:
2 tablespoons Dijon mustard or other good
quality French mustard
salt and white pepper
4 tablespoons wine vinegar
200 ml (⅓ pint) groundnut oil
1 teaspoon chopped fresh coriander leaves
1 teaspoon chopped chives

1 Put a saucepan containing enough water to cover the asparagus over high heat. Add the salt and bring the water to the boil.

2 Meanwhile, peel the base ends of the asparagus, about 5 cm (2 inches), preferably with a potato peeler. Tie the asparagus in equal, individual-sized bundles using fine string or cotton.

3 Add the bundles containing the largest asparagus to the boiling water first and cook for 2-3 minutes, then add the remaining bundles. Simmer white or mauve asparagus for 18-20 minutes. If you are using green asparagus from the United States or South Africa, less cooking time will be required. To test for tenderness, lift a few stalks at random and insert a knife. If the asparagus flesh feels soft, they are cooked. To arrest further cooking without breaking the asparagus tips, place the pan under gently running cold water for a few minutes or wrap a towel over the cold tap so that the water runs gently through the towel on to the asparagus.

4 While the asparagus spears are cooling, make the dressing. Put the mustard into a bowl with salt and pepper to taste, and stir well. With a wooden spatula or whisk, add the vinegar and mix thoroughly. Whisking rapidly, gradually add the oil, a small amount at a time. It is important to whisk well between each addition of oil to obtain an even consistency. When all the oil has been incorporated stir in the chopped coriander leaves and the chopped chives. Transfer the vinaigrette dressing to a sauce boat or jug.

5 Carefully drain the asparagus for a few minutes, then cut off the string from each bundle. The asparagus may either be arranged on a single serving dish so that guests can help themselves or on individual plates. Offer the vinaigrette separately.

ASPERGES DE BRÉTIGNY

Fʟᴀɢᴇᴏʟᴇᴛs À ʟᴀ ᴄʀÈᴍᴇ *(LEFT)*
GRATIN DE POMMES DE TERRE À LA DIJONNAISE *(RIGHT)*

FLAGEOLETS À LA CRÈME
CREAMED FLAGEOLET BEANS

SERVES 4

800 g (1¾ lb) fresh or canned flageolet beans
1 tablespoon coarse salt
1 onion, peeled and stuck with 2 cloves
1 small bouquet garni
75 g (3 oz) butter
4 shallots, peeled and finely chopped
3 cloves garlic, crushed
1 tablespoon chopped fresh parsley, to garnish
SAUCE:
20 g (¾ oz) butter
20 g (¾ oz) plain flour
4 tablespoons milk
100 ml (3½ fl oz) double cream
salt and pepper

1 Shell the beans. Put them in a saucepan of water with the salt, onion and bouquet garni. Bring to the boil, lower the heat and simmer for 25-30 minutes. To test if the beans are tender, take one or two beans between your fingers and press; if they feel soft and springy they are cooked. Drain thoroughly. If using canned flageolets, drain them thoroughly.

2 Melt the butter in the clean pan. Add the shallots and sweat for 2-3 minutes. Add the garlic and flageolet beans, mix well and keep warm over very low heat, stirring occasionally to prevent sticking.

3 Make the sauce. Melt the butter in a saucepan. Add the flour and cook over low heat, stirring, for 4-5 minutes. Gradually add the milk, stirring vigorously to avoid the formation of lumps. Cook, stirring, for 5 minutes over low to medium heat until thickened. Remove from the heat and stir in the cream. Stir the sauce into the flageolet mixture and simmer for 7-8 minutes. Check the seasoning.

4 Transfer the creamy flageolet mixture to a serving dish and sprinkle with chopped parsley. This dish may be served with all kinds of meat but is especially suitable for lamb.

GRATIN DE POMMES DE TERRE À LA DIJONNAISE
POTATO GRATIN, DIJON-STYLE

SERVES 6

1.5 kg (3¼ lb) medium potatoes
2 tablespoons coarse salt
5 shallots, peeled and finely chopped
¾ tablespoon chopped fresh chervil
1½ tablespoons chopped chives
salt and pepper
100 ml (3½ fl oz) double cream
4 tablespoons lemon juice
2 tablespoons Dijon mustard
50 g (2 oz) Gruyère or Cheddar cheese, grated

1 Put the potatoes in a saucepan of salted water. Bring to the boil, lower the heat and simmer for 25-30 minutes until tender.

2 Refresh the potatoes under cold running water for 5 minutes, then peel and cut into thick slices. Place them in a bowl and add the shallots, chervil, chives and salt and pepper to taste. Whisk the cream, lemon juice and mustard together in a bowl, then add the potatoes and mix gently to coat the potatoes.

3 Butter a gratin dish and add the potato mixture. Sprinkle the Gruyère cheese on top. Cook in a preheated moderately hot oven, 200°C (400°F), Gas Mark 6 for about 30 minutes. Serve immediately.

GRATIN DE COURGE
PUMPKIN GRATIN

SERVES 6
1.75 kg (4 lb) pumpkin, peeled and seeded
5 large potatoes, peeled
750 ml (1¼ pints) water
2 onions, peeled and quartered
2 teaspoons coarse salt
100 g (4 oz) butter
75 g (3 oz) lean smoked bacon, cut into
lardoons
4 eggs, beaten
200 g (7 oz) Gruyère or Cheddar cheese, grated
25 g (1 oz) butter
25 g (1 oz) dried breadcrumbs

1 Roughly chop the pumpkin and potatoes. Put them in a saucepan with the onions and salt. Add the water, cover and cook over moderate heat for 35 minutes. Drain well in a colander, removing as much moisture as possible.

2 Melt 20 g (¾ oz) of the butter in a roasting dish over high heat. When hot, add the bacon and sweat for 3-4 minutes.

3 Meanwhile, press the pumpkin and potatoes through a sieve or purée in a blender or food processor. Pour into a bowl and add the remaining butter, the eggs and the cheese, mixing well.

4 Pour the mixture into the roasting dish with the bacon. Bake in a pre-heated hot oven, 230°C (450°F), Gas Mark 8 for 10 minutes. Sprinkle the breadcrumbs on top and return to the oven for 3-4 minutes to brown the topping. Serve immediately.

POIREAUX EN SAUCE BLANCHE
LEEKS IN WHITE SAUCE

SERVES 6
12 leeks
1 tablespoon coarse salt
SAUCE:
25 g (1 oz) butter
25 g (1 oz) plain flour
500 ml (18 fl oz) milk
salt and pepper
pinch ground nutmeg
1 chicken stock cube, crumbled

1 If the leeks have long green tops, remove the top third and use in another dish, such as leek and potato soup. Quarter the leeks lengthways from the centre to the top (each leek should still be attached at the base). Leave to soak in cold water for about 10 minutes to clean, then wash well.

2 Bring a large saucepan of water to the boil with the salt. Add the leeks and cook over fairly high heat for about 25 minutes. (All the leeks should be immersed in water.) Drain and refresh the leeks under cold running water for about 5 minutes. Drain thoroughly.

3 Make the sauce. Melt the butter in a saucepan over moderate heat. Add the flour and cook for about 2-3 minutes over low heat, stirring. Gradually add the milk, stirring well to obtain a smooth sauce. Add salt, pepper and nutmeg to taste. Finally stir in the stock cube and cook gently over low heat for about 10 minutes, stirring.

4 Arrange the leeks in an ovenproof dish and pour over the white sauce. Bake in a preheated moderately hot oven, 200°C (400°F), Gas Mark 6 for about 7-8 minutes.

GRATIN DE COURGE *(ABOVE)*
POIREAUX EN SAUCE BLANCHE *(BELOW)*

POTÉE DE LENTILLES BOURGUIGNONNE

POTÉE DE LENTILLES BOURGUIGNONNE
BURGUNDY LENTIL HOT POT

SERVES 4
250 g (9 oz) green or grey lentils
1 onion, peeled and stuck with 1 clove
1 bouquet garni
1 teaspoon coarse salt
100 g (4 oz) butter
5-6 rashers streaky bacon, diced
5 shallots, peeled and sliced
1 tablespoon plain flour
1 chicken stock cube, crumbled
salt and pepper
1 tablespoon chopped fresh chervil, to garnish

1 Soak the lentils in cold water for 2-3 hours to soften. Drain thoroughly. Measure the volume of lentils in a measuring jug, then measure 2½ times the quantity of cold water. Put the lentils in a large saucepan and cover with the measured cold water. Bring to the boil over high heat. Add the onion and bouquet garni and cook over moderate heat for about 1 hour, adding the salt halfway through cooking. Drain the lentil mixture, reserving 200 ml (⅓ pint) of the stock.

2 Melt the butter in a pan over high heat. When the butter browns, add the bacon and fry for 7-8 minutes. Reduce the heat to moderate, add the shallots and sweat for about 2-3 minutes.

3 Sprinkle over the flour, mix thoroughly and slowly add the reserved lentil stock, stirring constantly. Cook for 5 minutes over moderate heat, then add the stock cube, drained lentil mixture and salt and pepper to taste. Cook for a further 2-3 minutes over low heat. Sprinkle with chopped chervil and serve.

GÂTEAU DE CÉLERI BRANCHE
CELERY SOUFFLÉ

SERVES 6
1.5 kg (3¼ lb) celery
2 teaspoons coarse salt
50 g (2 oz) butter, melted
salt and pepper
½ teaspoon finely chopped fresh coriander
5 eggs, separated
100 g (4 oz) Gruyère or Cheddar cheese, grated

1 Separate the celery sticks and, with a potato peeler, peel off any strings. Roughly chop the sticks and cut the heart into quarters.

2 Put the celery in a saucepan with water to just cover. Add the salt. Cook over high heat for 15 minutes. When tender, drain and refresh under cold running water. Leave to cool and when cold, drain the celery thoroughly in a colander.

3 Purée the celery in a blender or food processor. Transfer the celery purée to a bowl and add the butter, salt and pepper to taste, the coriander, egg yolks and cheese, mixing well so that all the ingredients are thoroughly blended. Whisk the egg whites until stiff, then gently fold into the celery mixture.

4 Grease a large soufflé dish and add the celery mixture. Bake in a pre-heated moderately hot oven, 190°C (375°F), Gas Mark 5 for 18-20 minutes until puffed and golden on top. Serve immediately.

DESSERTS AND BAKING

Having provided a feast of soups, hors-d'oeuvre, fish, meat, poultry and vegetables, the Burgundian cook continues her *tour de force* with her desserts and pastries. Batter puddings are a favourite, filled with fruit of various kinds, and fruit is used again in exquisite desserts like *Poires William Pochés au Vin Rouge* and *Tarte aux Pommes Caramelisées*. There are old-fashioned waffles, lightly sugared, and, to accompany tea or coffee, spicy breads of ancient tradition, like *Pain d'Épices*.

FLAMUSSE BOURGUIGNONNE
APPLE BATTER PUDDING

SERVES 4
90 g (3½ oz) butter
4 dessert apples, peeled, cored, quartered and
roughly chopped
40 g (1½ oz) plain flour
4 eggs
40 g (1½ oz) caster sugar
250 ml (8 fl oz) milk
2 tablespoons caster sugar to decorate

1 Melt 75 g (3 oz) of the butter in a saucepan and cook over high heat until nut brown. Add the apples, lower the heat and cook gently for 5 minutes, stirring from time to time to prevent the apples sticking.

2 Meanwhile, sift the flour into a bowl. Add the eggs, one at a time, and mix well. Stir in the sugar. Gradually add the milk, a little at a time, and stir until smooth. Finally, add the stewed apples.

3 Butter an ovenproof gratin or soufflé dish, using the remaining butter, and pour in the prepared mixture. Bake in a pre-heated moderately hot oven, 190°C (375°F), Gas Mark 5, for 30-35 minutes. Sprinkle with caster sugar and serve hot or warm.

CLAFOUTIS
CHERRY BATTER PUDDING

SERVES 6
750 g (1½ lb) cherries
90 g (3½ oz) plain flour
pinch salt
200 g (7 oz) caster sugar
4 eggs
750 ml (1¼ pints) milk
50 g (2 oz) butter

1 Remove the stalks from the cherries, wash and drain thoroughly. Traditionally, the stones are not removed from the cherries. This gives this dish its unique flavour and character. If, however, the dish is intended for young children, it would obviously be a good idea to remove the stones.

2 Sift the flour into a large bowl with the salt. Add 150 g (5 oz) of the sugar and incorporate the eggs, adding one at a time and mixing thoroughly with a wooden spoon. Gradually add the cold milk, stirring well to avoid the formation of lumps.

3 Butter a large oven-proof dish and arrange the cherries on the base. Cover with the batter. Bake in a preheated moderately hot oven, 200°C (400°F), Gas Mark 6, for 40 minutes. Remove from the oven, sprinkle with the remaining caster sugar and serve hot or warm. Offer extra sugar to sprinkle over the pudding, if liked. *Clafoutis* may be made with red or black cherries and also with wild ones. It may also be made with prunes or apples.

CLAFOUTIS

Tarte aux pommes caramelisées *(above)*
POIRES WILLIAM POCHÉS AU VIN ROUGE *(BELOW)*

POIRES WILLIAM POCHÉES AU VIN ROUGE
PEARS POACHED IN RED WINE

SERVES 6
6 William pears
1 litre (1¾ pints) red wine
1 glass Marc de Bourgogne (optional)
500 ml (18 fl oz) water
300 g (11 oz) sugar
1-2 sticks cinnamon
FRUIT PURÉE:
200 g (7 oz) raspberries
3 tablespoons water
200 g (7 oz) sugar
150 g (5 oz) blackcurrants
100 g (4 oz) redcurrants
juice of 1 lime

1 Peel the pears but leave the stalks on. Put the red wine, Marc, water, sugar and cinnamon in a saucepan. Bring to the boil, lower the heat, add the pears and simmer for 15-17 minutes, turning the pears from time to time. Remove the saucepan from the heat and allow the pears to cool in their juices for 2 hours.

2 Meanwhile, make the fruit purée. Combine the raspberries, water and sugar in a saucepan. Bring to simmering point and simmer for 10 minutes. Add the blackcurrants, redcurrants and lime juice and return to the boil. Lower the heat and simmer for 7-8 minutes, then pass the mixture through a very fine sieve into a bowl, discarding the skin and pips. Cool the purée for 2 hours, the last hour in the refrigerator.

3 Pour the purée into 6 dessert dishes so that it just covers the base. Place a pear in the centre of each dish with the stalk pointing upwards. Serve warm or cold.

TARTE AUX POMMES CARAMELISÉES
CARAMELIZED APPLE TART

SERVES 6
90 g (3½ oz) butter
200 g (7 oz) Pâte Brisée (shortcrust pastry, see page 76)
125 g (4½ oz) caster sugar
1.5 kg (3¼ lb) dessert apples, peeled, cored, halved and roughly sliced
150 g (5 oz) hazelnuts, chopped
juice of 2 limes
200 ml (⅓ pint) double cream, whipped (optional)

1 Butter a flan dish, using 15 g (½ oz) of the butter. Then roll out the pastry and line the dish. Prick the base with a fork and bake blind in a preheated moderate oven, 180°C (350°F), Gas Mark 4, for 20 minutes. Remove from the oven.

2 Melt the remaining butter in a frying pan over high heat, add the sugar and allow to caramelize lightly. Add the sliced apples and hazelnuts and cook over moderate heat for 20 minutes until the apples are thoroughly caramelized. Add the lime juice.

3 Reserve about one third of the apple slices, and pour the remainder into the flan case. Arrange the reserved slices in circles on top. Bake in a moderately hot oven, 200°C (400°F), Gas Mark 6, for 5 minutes. Then remove from the oven and put to one side to cool.

4 Slide the tart out of the dish and slice into six portions. Serve on dessert plates and decorate with whipped cream, if liked.

FLAN AU CASSIS
CURRANT FLAN

SERVES 4
500 g (1 lb) blackcurrants
200 g (7 oz) redcurrants
500 ml (18 fl oz) water
275 g (10 oz) caster sugar
2 leaves gelatine, dissolved in warm water
200 g (7 oz) Pâte Brisée (shortcrust pastry, see page 76)
4 tablespoons double cream

1 Put the blackcurrants and redcurrants in a saucepan and add the water. Bring to the boil, lower the heat and simmer gently for 8 minutes. Pass through a fine sieve into a saucepan, discarding the skin and pips.

2 Return the juice to the heat and add 250 g (9 oz) sugar and the gelatine. Bring back to the boil and then simmer gently for 25-30 minutes or until a few drops of juice dropped on to a plate, set. Remove from the heat.

3 Roll out the pastry and line a flan dish. Prick the base with a fork and bake blind in a preheated hot oven, 220°C (425°F), Gas Mark 7 for 5 minutes. Remove from the oven and pour the prepared currant juice into the flan case. Lower the oven temperature to 200°C (400°F), Gas Mark 6 and bake the flan for 30 minutes. Remove from the oven and leave in a cool place to set.

4 Stiffly whip the cream in a bowl, sprinkle with the remaining sugar and whip again to incorporate the sugar. Take the flan out of the dish and transfer to a serving plate. Decorate with the whipped cream, using a piping bag.

GAUFRES À LA BEAUJOLAISE
WAFFLES BEAUJOLAISE

SERVES 6-8
400 g (14 oz) plain flour
225 g (8 oz) vanilla sugar
6 eggs
1 tablespoon double cream
275 g (10 oz) butter, melted
1 teaspoon Marc de Bourgogne (optional)
oil for greasing iron
icing sugar, sifted, to decorate

1 Heat up the waffle iron while you prepare the batter.

2 Sift the flour into a bowl and add the vanilla sugar. Add the eggs one by one, beating thoroughly after each egg is added to avoid the formation of lumps. Stir in the cream, melted butter and, at the last minute, the Marc de Bourgogue.

3 When the waffle iron is hot, use a bristle brush to grease both sides of the plates with oil and pour a ladle of batter on to the flat dish, so it covers the surface and fills the design evenly. Be careful not to overfill. Then bring the lid down and cook for 2-3 minutes on each side.

4 Remove the waffle, transfer to a plate and keep warm.

5 Repeat the process until you have used up all the batter. Sprinkle the waffles lightly with icing sugar and serve immediately.

FLAN AU CASSIS *(ABOVE)*
GAUFRES À LA BEAUJOLAISE *(BELOW)*

POGNE BOURGUIGNONNE *(ABOVE)*
PAIN D'ÉPICES *(BELOW)*

POGNE BOURGUIGNONNE
RAISIN CAKE

SERVES 6
250 ml (8 fl oz) milk
20 g (¾ oz) fresh yeast
750 g (1½ lb) plain flour
4 eggs, beaten
125 g (4½ oz) caster sugar
150 g (5 oz) butter, softened
pinch salt
75 ml/3 fl oz rum
juice of 2 limes
grated rind of 1 lime
100 g (4 oz) raisins
2 egg yolks, diluted with a little water

1 Put the milk in a saucepan. Bring to the boil over high heat, allow to cool until just warm, then add the yeast.

2 Sift the flour into a large mixing bowl and make a well in the centre. Then add the eggs, the milk and yeast mixture, the sugar, 125 g (4½ oz) of the butter and the salt. Work the mixture with your hands until it is well mixed and has an elastic consistency. Then add the rum, lime juice, lime rind and raisins. Cover the bowl with a damp cloth and leave overnight in a warm place to rise.

3 The following morning, preheat the oven to moderate, 180°C (350°F), Gas Mark 4. Use the remaining butter to grease a baking sheet, and form the dough into a crown loaf shape. Brush the cake with diluted egg yolk and bake for 40-45 minutes or until the cake sounds hollow when tapped on the bottom. Serve warm.

PAIN D'ÉPICES
SPICE CAKE

MAKES ONE 20 CM (8 INCH) CAKE
375 g (13 oz) honey
200 ml (⅓ pint) milk
1 teaspoon vanilla essence
375 g (13 oz) wholemeal flour or equal
quantities wholemeal and rye flour
½ teaspoon salt
4 teaspoons baking powder
1½ teaspoons aniseed
2 teaspoons cinnamon

1 Combine the honey, milk and vanilla essence in a saucepan and heat gently until the honey has dissolved. Put the flour (or mixture of flours) in a mixing bowl with the salt. Make a well in the centre and add the honey mixture. Mix to a dough. Wrap in cling film and rest in the refrigerator for 1 hour.

2 On a floured work surface, knead the dough lightly, then work in the baking powder and spices. Line a 20 cm (8 inch) square baking tin with greaseproof paper and add the dough. Place an oiled sheet of greaseproof paper, oiled-side down, over the top of the mould, cover with foil and tie in place with string. (It is important not to omit this step; without the covering the cake would fall in the centre. In France a lidded tin would be used.)

3 Bake the cake in a preheated moderate oven, 180°C (350°F), Gas Mark 4 for 1 hour. Carefully remove the paper from the top of the tin and invert the cake on to a wire rack. Peel off the lining paper and allow the cake to cool. Serve cut in wedges or slices.

PÂTE À BRIOCHE
BRIOCHE DOUGH

MAKES 1 LARGE OR 4 SMALL BRIOCHES

150 g (5 oz) plain flour
120 g (4½ oz) butter
4 eggs
pinch salt
7 g (¼ oz) fresh yeast
pinch sugar (optional)
6 tablespoons warm milk

1 Sift the flour on to the work surface, make a well in the centre and add three-quarters of the butter, 2 eggs, the salt and the yeast, with the sugar if used. Mix together well, gradually adding the warm milk. Mix thoroughly, then add the remaining eggs, one at a time, and the rest of the butter. Form into a dough. Place the dough in a bowl, cover with a damp cloth and leave to rise in a warm place for 1-1½ hours, until doubled in bulk.

2 Knead the dough well on a lightly floured surface and work vigorously to knock out the air. Repeat the process 2 or 3 times.

3 Use the dough as desired. It may be shaped into a crown, baked in a fluted mould as 'brioche à tête' (with a small ball of dough on top), or used for small brioches. Alternatively, place the dough in a buttered rectangular mould, to half-fill the mould. Score the surface of the dough a few times to stop the brioche from splitting. Leave to rise again for about 1 hour, then bake in a preheated moderately hot oven, 200°C (400°F), Gas Mark 6, for 40-45 minutes. Turn out and cool.

PÂTE À CHOUX
CHOUX PASTRY

MAKES 200 G (7 OZ)
200 g (7 oz) plain flour
25 g (1 oz) caster sugar (for sweet pastry)
250 ml (8 fl oz) milk or water
150 g (5 oz) butter
pinch salt
6 eggs
salt and pepper (for savoury pastry)

1 Sift the flour on to a sheet of greaseproof paper. Add the sugar, if using. Put the milk or water into a saucepan with the butter and pinch of salt. Heat gently until the butter melts, then bring to the boil. Remove the pan from the heat and shoot in the flour (and sugar, if using) all at once. Beat vigorously. Return the pan to the heat and continue to beat until the mixture forms a ball, leaving the sides of the pan clean.

2 Off the heat, add the eggs one at a time, beating well between each addition. Add seasoning if the pastry is to be savoury, and beat for 2-3 minutes more until smooth and glossy. Use as desired.

PÂTE BRISÉE
SHORTCRUST PASTRY

Made without sugar, this pastry is ideal for savoury pies and quiches. With sugar, it may be used for sweet flans and tarts.

MAKES 250 G (9 OZ)
250 g (9 oz) plain flour
pinch salt
1 egg
25 g (1 oz) caster sugar (optional)
125 g (4½ oz) butter, softened
3 tablespoons water

1 Sift the flour on to the work surface and make a well in the centre. Add the salt and egg to the well, with the sugar if a sweet pastry is required. Add the butter, cut into small pieces. Using the fingertips, sprinkle on the water, adding a little at a time, and stir with a round-bladed knife until the mixture begins to stick together in large lumps. It should not be too wet. With your hands, quickly gather the dough together into a ball; avoid handling it too much. Wrap the pastry in cling film or foil and rest in the refrigerator for several hours, or overnight. It may be prepared a day or two in advance.

2 When the pastry is required, sprinkle a little flour on to a work surface and on to the rolling pin. Roll out evenly in one direction only, turning the pastry occasionally, until about 3 mm (⅛ inch) thick. Use as required.

P̂ÂTE BRISÉE *(LEFT)*
PÂTE À CHOUX *(ABOVE)*
PÂTE À BRIOCHE *(RIGHT)*

INDEX